ACCESS THE REAL YOU

*Touching Your Divinity
and Applying Its Wisdom to Your Life*

BRIAN KURTZ

ISBN: 979-8-218-16551-2 (print book)

Author: Brian Kurtz
Publisher: Healed By Spirit
Website: https://www.healedbyspirit.com/

The Real You/Brian Kurtz. First edition.

DEDICATION

I dedicate this book to the late Colin Lambert who, in the late 1990s, showed me what was possible in the realm of healing one's self and others. I'd just watched him facilitate a client walking across a friend's living room after twenty-five years in a wheelchair, and I asked him how he was accomplishing what looked like miracles, given that I was still working with people' knees, backs, and such. His answer was simple: "You just need to be a clearer vessel." This book points the way to that which is already in you that makes possible everything that your heart desires.

I also dedicate this book to all of the writers, musicians, and lovers of humanity whose lives, as the vessels they are, touch deeply all of us who resonate with that which pours out of their souls for us.

Lastly, I dedicate this book to my great grandmother, Dora Riseman, who, though having only a third grade education, was perhaps the most "tuned in," loving, and dynamic woman I've ever witnessed. Her life continues to bless me.

TABLE OF CONTENTS

WHY I'M WRITING THIS FOR YOU

I'm sharing this to give you an idea of where I came from, and what got me here. Please read this segment from this perspective. All of the following are the parts of my life that led to the learning experiences, which in turn led to the writing of this book.

I grew up as the Jewish kid in mostly Catholic south Louisiana, the buck-toothed kid, the short kid, the skinny kid, and every other reason people used to justify my getting physically and/or emotionally abused pretty much every day of my first twenty years of life. There were, of course, some good times . . . neighborhood ball games, my time in the Boy Scouts, during which I served in pretty much every important role a scout can involve himself in, including earning my Eagle Scout Award. I also played tournament-level tennis, bowled in leagues and tournaments with my dad, and was president of my local Southern Federation of Temple Youth group. Still, there was always that nagging and very persuasive voice in my head that convinced me I was unworthy and would never be quite good enough. I'd gathered enough evidence to be fairly certain I could never quite find real happiness, a sense of inclusion, or the romantic love that remained so elusive. Even more disconcerting was that what occurred around me consistently mirrored those thoughts in my brain. Those thoughts lived as a never-ending reminder in my brain, in my body, and in my life. I was always waiting for the disaster that lurked behind the next corner.

After college, I experienced failed marriages and, as a provider (an important mandate for us males out there), never got paid as much as

I was promised, despite blowing through every goal ever set in front of me. Problems surrounded me with my kids, ex-wives, workplace bosses; I thought of the whole world either being against me or, at best, never understanding me. I had stuff floating around in my head all day—some conscious, some unconscious—precious little of it productive, motivational, inspiring, or encouraging, and most of it counterproductive, depressing, and downright stifling. I tried my best to fit in everywhere I went, but even when I was succeeding, I still felt terribly insecure and alienated from pretty much every group with which I was involved. There's an old Groucho Marx quote that goes something like, "I would never belong to a club that would have me as a member." Indeed, I felt like "anyone who likes me must have even bigger issues than I do."

Even the good news never lasted very long. I felt like the proverbial lovable loser—I took great care of everyone around me and yet perceived little of it being reciprocated. By the time I'd been through my ex-wives, I'd at least learned how to be pleasing, so I had lots of success at attracting women but not so much success at keeping them around for more than a few years. Usually, they ended with me rejecting them before they could reject me . . . habituated thought processes grounded firmly in my consistent, history-based circumstances.

There were many jobs at which I excelled at the highest level. I was a recognized Exploring Executive with the Boy Scouts of America. For three years, I was a plaque-earning professional recreation programmer who was beloved by everyone in town. I even had my own weekly column in the newspaper. I was an outstanding regional sales trainer who tripled sales in three years and literally helped rebuild the company for which I was working. I did so well in that job that one of the companies I represented hired me to be their North American sales and training director, and again, I tripled sales in my three years there. Still, when it came time for the raise I'd been promised, I didn't have the foundational self-worth to insist I be paid well when the time arrived that I be paid as promised. I finally left feeling disrespected (now realizing I didn't respect myself enough to receive what I'd certainly earned) and bullied by the bosses there.

I then started a retail business that, after about a decade, was finally starting to take off, until the Great Recession buried my business. I was distraught on my good days, and on my bad days the only things that kept me from extensive suicidal musings were my never-ending desire to care for my sons and the love and appreciation of the few clients and friends who'd reached out to see if I was still around.

After years of failing in my work, failing at my marriages, and failing in my other romantic relationships, I finally reached a bottom. It was at this bottom that something finally shifted. Reaching bottom had placed me in a position of having to not just endure, but to finally learn a new and better way of being. Maybe, instead of pushing harder and harder I could work smarter. Maybe instead of seeing a trail of failed jobs and failed relationships, I could study what had happened and figure out what I could do differently that might work better. I began to dig into my history, not as a vehicle for justifying self-deprecation and self-loathing, but as something to be examined from a stepped-back, nose-off-the-grindstone perspective; that was more objective than subjective in nature. I shifted from self-deprecation to self-study. I also came to realize—as in to "make real" for myself—that *who I was being* had become a far bigger problem than *what I was doing*. I could see I'd been living in fear-based anger, frustration, and self-loathing, distrusting everyone around me and distrusting myself. I had lost all confidence in my ability to wisely choose a job or a romantic partner, and was even losing trust in myself regarding ever living a happy life.

Finally, almost to the day that I'd given up hope on any future in the world of business or much of anything else, I got a message from a woman I knew from the church I'd been attending, who suggested I come to a "Mastermind" group—a gathering of like-minded folks who agree to hear and support each other in what means most to them—centered around determining one's next career path. Turned out the meeting was only a few blocks from where I lived, so how could I not notice that synchronicity? I went, and the leader, a brilliant life coach named David Cantu, after giving us the introductory details, said "Who wants to lead off?" I raised my hand, and he asked, "OK, Brian, so what do you want to do with the rest of your life?"

"I want to be a healer."

"A healer? What do you mean by that?"

"Well, I have this gift that when people come to me with pretty much any sort of physical condition, I see a visualization and some hand gestures to do, and I do those. I see energy leaving their bodies and more energy going in, and they're almost always better, often immediately."

"You can DO THAT?!"

"Well, I'm not actually the one doing the work. God/Spirit/Creator or whatever you want to call that thing is doing the work."

"So why aren't you already doing that?! That's incredible!!!!"

"Well, what if people come to me with chronic digestive issues, or kidney failure, or something?!"

"I thought you said God was doing the work! Why don't you get out of the way and let God do the work?"

As the words came out of his mouth, I felt my entire life shift, like trying to stand up in an 8.0 earthquake. Why *not* let God do the work? At that moment I figured that if I dedicated my life to doing healing work, I still might not get paid much, but at least it would be very rewarding. And best of all, I was no longer the one responsible for generating a positive result. I literally, in that moment, handed my life and career off to God—not "God," like a guy up in heaven with a long white beard who dispenses good fortune or punishment like a vending machine—but *the God in me*. In the words of Fr. Richard Rohr, "being vulnerable and transparent allows that Divine Power to come *through us as us*" for the people in front of us!

In that instant, I handed off "cause" to something far bigger, far more loving, and far more permanent than I was or would ever be. That moment was the beginning of an adventure that, despite more troubles, more confusion, and more disappointments, has taught me what I'm about to present to you in this book.

The point? That there's something bigger than my well-considered, judged-by-my-brain-to-be-a-thoroughly-proven-by-historical-evidence-to-be-hopeless life. I learned to be guided, as I'd always been guided during all of my healing sessions, by something greater than my physical brain and body. Now I was beginning to apply this inner "Capital K Knowing" to every aspect of my life! I was now learning the beginnings of what has evolved into what I call The Real You principles.

I discovered (as in uncovered something that was always there) that part of me which is bigger than any circumstances I will ever encounter, stronger than any weakness I might otherwise personally claim, and is a more permanent state of Beingness than even my physical existence itself. Let me be clear—*this is not about religion.* This book presents a common-sense, practical, applicable process guided by simple principles that leads to accessing The Real You—that part of us that few ever know beyond a brain-understood concept, and even fewer can access readily as needed. This book is about granting you ready access to your own inherent divinity—that part of you that is tied to something far greater than you and your physical existence, to which you are inexorably tied, and which sources every aspect of your life, your health, and your capacity for unconditional love and self-love, forgiveness and self-forgiveness, which drives your very self-evolution.

Ready to learn the way to this magical way of living? Read on, dear one.

Brian Kurtz

CHAPTER ONE

WHY THIS BOOK?

I request that you read this book with what I call "vacation eyes." Like when you go somewhere and your internally generated enthusiasm and eager anticipation allow even the most familiar places to feel fresh and new and stimulating? Yeah! That! You may have "heard it all before," but I'm willing to bet you've not heard it presented in quite this way. I call it "accessible woo-woo."

I want you to know where the guy writing this book came from, what I had to endure and work through (not like that ever actually ends), and to know from the outset that at the heart of it all, I'm just another human being like you who's learned the most valuable lessons in life. Part of me wishes I'd learned these sooner but, at soul level, I know that it really and truly is "better late than never," and that the part of us that we usually allow to determine "better/worse," "early/late," "good/bad," and "worthy/unworthy" is precisely the problem. We'll cover that later.

My hope is that the principles presented herein touch you in ways that are both powerful and *permanent*. Once everyone realizes (as in, "to make real" for themselves) that all we ever really need already lives within us (possibly sleeping, but alive, I assure you!), the self-help industry is history. Once we realize that anything we notice—the thoughts our brains are generating, what's happening in our bodies, or even what we witness in the world around us—can all be your own self-generating, never-ending, ever-present teaching material, at that very moment your very own mind, your very own body, and your very own life experiences become your very own greatest teachers.

The principles presented herein and the structure of the presented materials, once learned and practiced, contain all you'll ever need to show you how to more effectively, more powerfully, and more purposefully navigate your life. You will soon, with practice, build within you a resilience you may never before have possessed or even considered possible. You won't need to "endure" any longer. You'll learn to *live.* My goal, quite simply, is that this is the last self-help book you'll ever need, because unlike most self-help books that start from the false assumption that you need something outside yourself that "they" are going to give you, this book is all about giving you ready access to something *already inside of you,* that's always been there, waiting for you to consistently and courageously access *on demand.* These are simple principles with surprisingly (from where you might now be standing) creative and transformative power. Simple, though not necessarily easy, and always available.

I truly believe there's nothing more important than soul work, and that nothing is more important to the survival of our shared planet than everyone connecting deeply, which is another result that becomes available from reading this book. This book is all about helping you access you own soul, touching that special place more readily, and supporting you and everyone around you in connecting more deeply with yourself and everyone you meet at that soul level place where all the fun happens!

This is the place where love happens. It's the place from where music and poetry flow, pouring out from our hearts and touching others' hearts. It's always in there in large measure, like a 300-foot column of water on the other side of a dam that you've unknowingly erected through your own accumulated life experiences up to now, which will soon come flooding over your life in ways that will touch every part of your life to which you grant yourself access. The flood of internal power that becomes available will wash away the usual troubles, concerns, habits, and compensatory behaviors with a speed and power that may leave you wondering, "what the heck has happened to me?" Every aspect of your life to which you apply The Real You principles will become more effortlessly fulfilling, more consistently manageable, more powerfully productive, and more palpably *real.*

Two thousand years ago, a guy named Jesus is said to have claimed "the Kingdom of Heaven lies within." If this is so, then we need nothing outside of ourselves to be and act heavenly. So what happened? Remember that "original sin" story? That is what happened. Later in the book, I'll give you my take on the whole Adam and Eve and "original sin" thing, and why I so very strongly disagree with the way organized religion has interpreted this story. The bottom line is that we all have unconditional ready access to the divine within us. The problem for most of us is accessing it and more readily and easily operating from that place of unity consciousness, nonattachment, nonjudgment, and nonduality. This book is all about how to do that more effortlessly and naturally than you've ever thought possible.

When you learn how to connect to yourself at the level of your own soul, a lot of magic becomes available. If you've ever watched a magic show, there's a way the magician does what the magician does that makes the audience believe for that precious moment that something incredible is happening. But it's not really magic to the magician. We can be fascinated at the fact that the magician's illusions appear quite real, but we know all the while that there are specific techniques required to make it all happen. The art of accessing your own soul, connecting with others at this soul-level, and the life possibilities arising from the art and science of this process may seem like magic. But I assure you that unlike the magician's magic, this "magic" is real! The best part is that once you experience and practice the techniques presented in this book and really get grounded in them, the apparent magic of living an invincible and joy-filled life will always be available to you. There will be no circumstances able to take you down. None of life's problems—even the ones that seem insurmountable now—will be more than you can handle. Nothing will be able to stop you, and nothing will be able to prevent you from being happy, healthy, and consistently more self-actualized.

Here's the best part, repeated: what you'll "receive" from this book is already within you. Your successes that will most certainly come from practicing what you'll learn in this book will happen, not from obtaining something you think you need that you didn't already have, but from accessing what you already have that has always been inside you. Maybe you haven't realized you've had it all along or maybe you've had it and believed you'd lost it (I certainly had no clue it was in there!). But it is in there, and you'll soon have ready access to it whenever you need it. The difference between being in flow and not being in flow is the degree to which you can free yourself of the stuff that's in the way of all you already are and all you already have inside you. This is one of what I call The Real You principles: *When you release all that's in the way, what remains is who you are.*

First of all, you'll learn how to "get there." The tricky part is that the way there is really counterintuitive, because the nature of being is not really something you can easily put your finger on. But once you experience it—and I'm assuming perhaps you already have, or maybe you haven't to the extent you might prefer—there are times when "you know that you know." Those are the moments I'm talking about.

Second, you'll learn what to do and, more importantly, *who to be* when you get there. We're not naturally culturally tuned in to the way that's required, and the world gives us precious little to go on that helps us be the way that's required. Still, once you read it here and, most of all, when you begin practicing it, you'll be amazed at how your life transforms.

The apostle Paul (again, this isn't religion, I'm just quoting an appropriate passage—I'm not even really a fan of most of what Paul wrote to the congregants at churches he established) mentioned in one of his letters a "peace that passes understanding." What I believe he meant by this is there's a place to which we have access that the brain can't fully comprehend, yet the brain "knows that it knows" it's experiencing that peace, certainty, and stillness when it's happening. There's that "Knowing" that's the "you know that you know" place beyond the brain's ability to the drop the experience into a categorizable and understandable place. To access that place I call The Real You— that place beyond one's brain's understanding—requires we get past the brain's need to understand the wholeness of every encountered phenomenon (which can never really be accomplished in the first place), to see it with certainty and to notice in the moment, standing in The Real You place, that the brain is holding whatever it experiences within an inherently false context of expectation and familiarity. The nature of Being is that we can't really completely describe It. The word for an experience or thing that's beyond words is "ineffable." If the ineffable sounds inaccessible, it's not (here's where you may toss this book before you really get started), but it *is* something not easily labelled beyond one's present-moment experience of it. This book is about getting past the brain's reasons, justifications, and "becauses," and its need for certainty and familiarity that it otherwise requires. This book is about getting beyond these inherently experience-limiting thought structures to the deeper, eternally present, and transcendent knowing that's available in your heart and your gut, and which is available at any time.

There's a group called the Institute for Heart Math, and they've done decades of study around this heart-gut neural network, which actually is known to have 5,000 times more electromagnetic energy than the brain's neural network. They've also learned that this neural network is sending out more information up to the brain than the brain is sending down to what many call, "the second brain."

When I heard this "5,000 times thing," I called up one of my clients, who's also one of my healer's class students, who had for many years earned her living as a cardio-stenographer. Her job was to generate and read (not analyze, that's the cardiologist's job) the tape off the EKG machine. She said, "Oh yeah! 5,000 times? For sure!"

As she described it to me, an EEG machine is basically the same as an EKG machine, except that if you hook your brain up to an EKG machine, it likely wouldn't register anything. If you hooked your heart up to an EEG machine, the magnitude of the measured charge would fry the circuitry. That's not really where we're going, but I wanted to be able to touch on this because I believe this "second brain" is far more useful to us than we might otherwise be aware. And awareness is the key. Not an awareness that you *have*, as much as the awareness that you *are*.

You may now be asking, "What? Huh?"

Let's look at it from a different angle. If I were to ask you, "Who do you love?" what would be your answer? You might answer, "I love my cat." Notice that your brain instantly generates all the reasons to justify your knowing that your cat is lovable . . . the cat's cute (or not so cute, but tolerable because you love your kitty) habits, way of eating, or begging, or being lovable, or the way he/she hops into any box you put on the floor, or the way he/she sits on your computer's keyboard at exactly the time you're about to start working. We all know that list of lovable attributes, right? Beyond that, however, is that Knowing that you already and always just know that you know. There's that place where you know that you know you love your kitty—beyond the reasons and beyond the brain-generated comparisons and justifications. There's an important piece to notice in differentiating between "the brain that knows" and that part of you that knows that it knows beyond what the brain is generating about it.

That "you know that you know" place is where I'm going to take you in this book and, with practice, where you will be foundationally, immovably, and confidently planted. When we're done, I promise you that you'll have ready access to The Real You place—the place beyond a brain-generated and brain-required certainty. You'll be able to easily get there anytime, anywhere, in any circumstance, especially (with practice) in those times when you most need clarity, insight, and that foundational and immutable level of peaceful steadiness amid any turmoil you may be facing.

Please understand that I'm not suggesting that you stop using your brain. You'll still need your brain for navigating your way around town, to read your home budget pages or corporate balance sheet, or to calculate measurements for your favorite recipe, etc. Here's the point: When you come to the fork in the road, you need to know, using your brain, "Do I turn left here, or do I turn right here? Then, when I've done that, how far do I go before my next turn?" etc. When you come to the forks in the road of *life,* however, you're really much better off letting your guidance come from a place beyond reasons, justifications, and concerns and from the place of Knowing You Know.

As I write this, our world is still working through the global COVID pandemic, and many feel we are collectively politically, socially, ethically, and economically going to hell in a hand basket. Everyone's nerves are raw, and everybody's yelling and screaming and freaking out and blocking friends on social media. Anyone who's even slightly aware is fed up with all the misinformation and disinformation floating around, the polarization of so many aspects of daily life, and the stress and uncertainty and alienation that comes from it all.

It's enough to drive anyone insane, right? Yes, until you get grounded in what's in this book, which will remind you of who you are regardless of your current circumstances. The Real You principles won't change the circumstances but will radically alter who you're being about them. You'll be able to witness the madness, and it won't affect you as strongly as perhaps it's been affecting you. Another note: if all of this madness *has* had an effect on you, that's a prompt, as it were, to notice that. Not to let it take you down the proverbial rabbit hole . . . just to notice it.

What I want you to do is to read and integrate what we cover in this book and *practice it* (are you getting the feeling that I really mean it when I ask you to practice this stuff you're going to read about?). I'm going to give you some legitimately accessible and powerful ways to become so grounded in that part of you that is beyond circumstances, preferences, desires, and expectations—The Real You—that you will become virtually impervious to the "stuff of the day" that might otherwise take you down that possibly-familiar rabbit hole of anger, sadness, disappointment, hopelessness, despair, stress, and pain. Here's the coolest part: *all of that stuff will still be there, but you'll be able to consistently and progressively more easily rise above it*! You'll accomplish this, not by denying it, not by avoiding it, not by reframing it, or many of the temporarily effective ways you've likely been shown, or which your brain has figured out over the years. All of these are, after all, just coping mechanisms that will never really affect who you're being about it all. By learning how to stand in what I realize will be for many an entirely new place, however, you will come to know that grounded, truly stable and foundational place that will always be bigger, stronger, and more powerful than any circumstances in which you may find yourself. No more feeling frightened, trapped, or helpless. No more desperation, resignation, and hopelessness. The Real You will be The Real *YOU*.

Another beautiful thing to know about this learning and practice is that it's frightfully *simple*. It may not be *easy* at first, because we're not wired up to do the practice. But it's eminently doable by pretty much anyone willing to stick with it. You'll get glimpses, then epiphanies, and finally you'll be walking it, applying The Real You principles to every aspect of your life.

Look around you. The world is, for the most part, run by people I'd wager have never had this sort of discussion or read this sort of book. Turmoil is all around us, and most have no clue how to extricate themselves from it. Is there any wonder we have a mental health crisis in our society? Is there any wonder we are the most medicated and self-medicated society on the planet? Even if folks aren't smoking as much heavily chemically-laden tobacco products these days, many are now inhaling dangerous "vape" products that may yet generate another national health crisis in the decades to come. If folks aren't consuming alcohol and various chemical compounds for any number of mental, emotional, and physical conditions—most of which are advertised on our various media all day long—they're partaking of legal and/or illegal products to numb the pain.

"THERE MUST BE A BETTER WAY!" we exclaim.

Fortunately, there is a better way, and this book is written to provide you with just that. This book is not a new excuse or justification to placate you into thinking life's OK when it's not. It's not a new bunch of positive slogans so you can "fake it 'til you make it." It's not some way to dumb down or numb out, or deny, or suppress what you know you're thinking and feeling.

This book will provide you with a new way of being about all of it. This book provides tools and perspectives that, when practiced diligently and implemented on an ongoing basis, will literally transform your life and bring you to a new place beyond your circumstances. You'll soon be in a place beyond your troubled mind's exhausting attempts at figuring a way out of the chasm in which you most feel trapped. You'll begin to transcend even the physical maladies that befall most who have lived for decades with the relentless pressures of just surviving in this world. I know these are lofty promises, but by the time you finish this book and practice what is presented herein, you will join the thousands of people already touched and moved by its teachings in my classes and workshops that have been presented for the last several years.

For the record, the contents of this book have come through me, not from me, for you. When I talk about accessing The Real You, I'm talking about accessing that part of us that is beyond the physical yet is what sources the physical. We'll get to that in a bit, but know that part will be covered in greater detail. Every single one of us is a unique soul, and each of us possesses, in our inherent divinity, our individuated expression within a spiritual Whole, which Dr. David Hawkins called our "Eachness in the Allness." We are One within the collective "All That Is," yet we are as individual as our physical fingerprints, retina scans, and DNA will surely indicate.

The universal applicability of this book's contents will, I hope, positively impact the planet. Applying these universal principles to your unique life situation and circumstances will, I hope, guide you to a place where you literally become not just "tough enough" to endure what may befall you, but impervious to anything your life may hand you; to provide you with access to your own innate courage, providing you with a level of consistent and confidence-building resilience to not just rise above it all as circumstances occur, but to stand in a place that puts you above it all even before anything happens.

My goal in writing this book is an ambitious one: to positively impact the planet for the better forever. How close we come is up to each of us. Thanks for allowing that which is in you to move you to purchase and read this book and to practice what's here for you so you can be That Which is Most You, no matter what.

Again, what differentiates this book from most self-help publications is that most of them are not actually self-help, but, "Let me help you by showing you something you don't have that you need to achieve, do, and be x, y, z." As I've already mentioned (but want to make sure it sinks in), *Access The Real You* presents a perspective that allows you to access, awaken, and maintain a relationship with what's already in you, as well as a way to access, awaken, and notice with The Real You what's going on in your mind, in your body, and what's occurring around you, and have those become your teachers and your teaching material. This is not a bunch of cool-sounding platitudes or affirmations to keep reciting to yourself, which you may or may not even believe, but actual, practical access to all you already are. I want you to know way down into your bones that what's available there is not just enough, it is plenty. *You. Are. Plenty. Already.* Nothing else required for health, happiness, prosperity, and relationships that you've always dreamed about having.

The resulting self-generating, self-inspiring, self-forgiving, and self-loving way of being will deposit you into the place to which you have always had access such that you will never again feel lacking in any way in any life aspect.

I know. You're already saying, "But what if I slip?"

Know that we all slip, and when you slip, you will have the easy-to-access tools and, I promise you, the wherewithal to once again stand in the place beyond anything you may encounter, because there's nowhere to go and nothing to get that you don't already have. It's all in there. Trust me. I've been there, upside and downside, and I am, even now, on the ongoing journey of living my best life, having made more mistakes than I can ever count, and I'm still working through some of them, which were once completely and depressingly overwhelming, and are now manageable pieces of a whole.

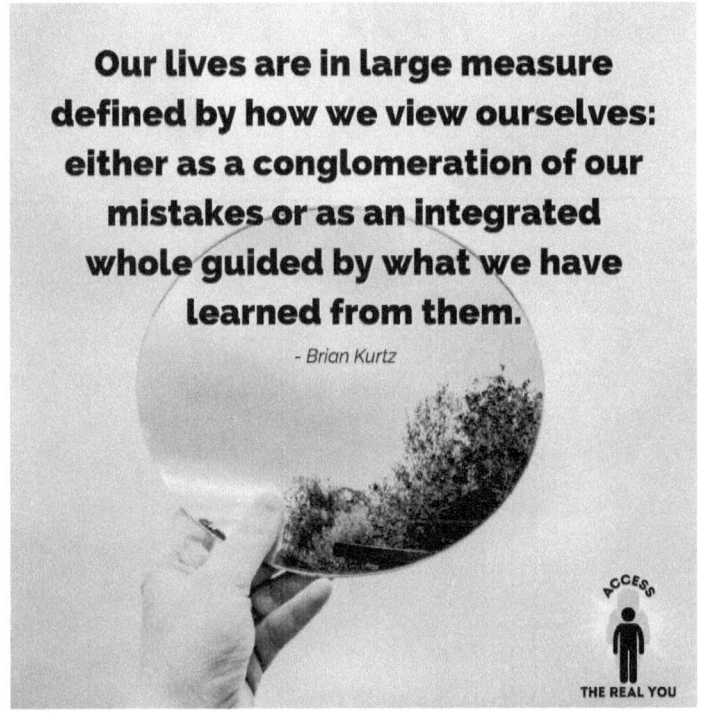

Our lives are in large measure defined by how we view ourselves: either as a conglomeration of our mistakes or as an integrated whole guided by what we have learned from them.

- Brian Kurtz

ACCESS
THE REAL YOU

Using a book analogy, your story is not over. What you thought was your life may now be seen as just pages within a chapter, and that you are, in fact, able to write new chapters toward the happiest ending you can imagine! My life has changed forever for the better by what's come through me for you in this book. If you're ready to live a life in the way that is You Being Most You, free of anything which might otherwise prevent you from doing and being that, read on!

CHAPTER TWO

"I AM NOTICING THE THOUGHTS MY BRAIN IS GENERATING"

Our bodies are made up of many vital organs—heart, lungs, kidneys, liver, pancreas, and others—each of which has a very specific job to do. What makes a "vital organ" vital is that if it stops working, we have a limited time remaining, in which one of two things must happen

- We get that organ repaired or replaced, or
- We're done here on earth

Obvious, right? Here's another obvious point: the brain is a vital organ that controls to some extent many of the others. Before we go into too detailed an anatomical discussion, let's say we understand at some level the usual discussed complexities of the brain and, for the purpose of this book, rein in the discussion to a more practical point: *the brain is the vital organ in the body that pumps out thought.* As the heart pumps blood, the lungs pump air, and the stomach pumps out digestive acids, our brains pump out thoughts. All day, every day, as long as we're alive and until we're gone.

Let's notice, for a moment, what the brain is up to. The brain processes stimuli of various sorts and immediately figures out how any and all aspects of observed stimuli tie together in any way it can create—comparisons of "this to that," ponderings of where, when, how, why, and what, etc., and the brain will either "sit and simmer" on that for a while, or it may be off to whatever you may perceive next. This process becomes more obvious when one considers what occurs when we see a billboard as we drive down the expressway. On the billboard we notice images, words, colors, logos, and other symbols. All of these trigger thoughts related to those images, words, colors, and symbols, such as songs or long lost sweet memories that may be evoked. Memories of happy times similar to the ones portrayed on the billboard may awaken feelings about our own experiences, and we might actually feel better about life in general simply from seeing a billboard for a few seconds. The more readily the billboard is able to elicit a predicted/hoped-for set of thoughts and feelings, the more readily remembered that billboard's sponsor will be, leading to more sales or at least increased name recognition for that sponsor.

Obvious bottom line: Folks who market to you know how your brain works and specifically choose images, colors, logo designs, and verbiage designed to evoke responses, memories, etc., whether consciously or subconsciously.

Not-so-obvious bottom line and another one of The Real You principles: *You are not your brain, you are the noticer of it.*

It starts with noticing. What I want you to notice is that you *can* notice that.

I want you to repeat a sentence back to me. Just speak it out loud. Ready? I know you're reading a book . . . just play along, OK? Here we go.

"I'm noticing the thoughts my brain is generating."

OK, now repeat it (please keep playing along, and say it out loud).

"I'm noticing the thoughts that my brain is generating."

GOOD!

So, who is the "I" that you just mentioned that's noticing the thoughts *your* brain is generating? I? Me? My soul? My consciousness?

All of those are good answers. The point is, there is an "I" that you can identify that is noticing the thoughts your brain is generating. It's as if there's an "I" standing right here, next to your brain and body, that's noticing the thoughts your brain is generating, and that "I" is quite possibly distinct from your brain and your body.

Here's the next piece: When you are being the noticer of the thoughts your brain is generating, this not only points out that there is an "I" that can be the noticer of the thoughts your brain is generating, it also begs the next question, "*Where* is the 'I' that is noticing the thoughts that your brain is generating?"

Now, there may not really be a physical location for that entity we're distinguishing, but clearly it is located outside the brain where it can be the noticer of the thoughts your brain is generating. So, I want you to notice that there is an "I," and that "I" is what I call *The Real You*. It's "the you that's really you," as distinct from the "you" that's nothing more than the thoughts your brain is generating. It's also distinct from the body that has a brain in it that's generating the thoughts! The Real You is not your brain, nor is it the body that has a brain in it pumping out thought. Get that? *The Real You is the noticer of the thoughts your brain is generating, the noticer of what's happening in your body, and the noticer of everything that's occurring around you.*

When you start to notice that you can notice what you're noticing; you're going to notice that you have thoughts and thoughts about the thoughts; and thoughts about the thoughts about the thoughts; and judgments and evaluations about the thoughts about the thoughts about the thoughts. And soon you're going to notice, "GEEZ! My brain is moving a thousand miles an hour all day!" That's correct, and there's more! Our brains are moving a thousand miles an hour even when we're asleep! How do I know this? I'm sure you've had dreams that felt like they lasted three hours, but you woke up, checked the clock, and it's only two minutes later? We've probably all had this experience, correct? Your brain is moving so fast, especially when you're asleep, it's almost like it's managed to stop time!

An issue arises about which I'm working on forgiving myself, and I find I'm not as self-forgiving about it as I'd prefer.

WAIT! I'M NOT FORGIVING MYSELF BECAUSE I'M NOT BEING SELF-FORGIVING ENOUGH?!?!?!

HOW RIDICULOUS IS THAT?!

Yet this is what we do.

Until we truly know that the "I" that judges is not The Real You.

Be the Noticer of the judgment. That's The Real You.

- Brian Kurtz

ACCESS
THE REAL YOU

Here's the point: you are not your brain. The Real You is the noticer of your brain. And here's another fascinating part: when you are noticing that your brain is moving a thousand miles an hour, the you that's really you—The Real You, when it's being the noticer—is, by definition, in a place of stillness (pause for effect) noticing your brain moving a thousand miles an hour.

Let that sink in. When you're noticing that your brain is moving a thousand miles an hour, the you that's really you—The Real You, when it's being the noticer—is by definition, in a place of *stillness,* noticing your brain moving a thousand miles an hour.

Are you somewhat confused? Cut yourself some slack! Remember, you've been doing this identified-with-your-brain thing your entire life, and you're now just a few pages into this book, being shown a different way. Breathe into it. It gets easier, I promise!

The counterintuitive part of this process is that everyone wants to be in that stillness place. We all need to be in that place for at least a short while every day. After all, there's so much weighing us down every day—turmoil in the world, turmoil at work, tension at home, stress and challenges in our relationships with friends and family—and our brains are attempting to find solutions and certainty amid all of the turmoil or at least a safe quiet place to process it all. So, what do we do? Maybe you've tried getting there through meditation or breathing exercises, or a host of other different things. We're going to cover those, and I'm going to give you some really effective and practical ways to get you there. For now, however, what I want you to notice is that The Real You—the place of that so-very-strongly-desired stillness—is accessed by being the noticer of your brain, which is generally not in stillness.

This is another one of The Real You principles: *you access stillness by noticing what is not stillness.* You access silence by noticing the noise all around you, from the noticer place I call The Real You.

When you're noticing, you are accessing the place you're seeking! When you're being the noticer, you're stepping back and separating The Real You from the brain's incessant chatter and grounding yourself in another separate, noticer place.

People come to me regularly and say, "Brian, I can't slow my brain down! I can't meditate! I can't relax! I'm FREAKING OUT! I remind them that it's totally OK that your brain is freaking out, because you are not your brain, you are the noticer of it! In other words, The Real You is not the one freaking out! Your brain is the one freaking out! It's totally fine if you can't stop your brain. It's a vital organ in your body, remember?! You don't want it to stop because that likely means you're dead! What you really want is control over the stress, the massive amount of brain chatter, and the worldly mess that we slog through all day, right?

At this very moment, your brain is generating the "who and how you are" that's reading this book. As you're reading this, you might notice that your brain is judging, evaluating, analyzing, and categorizing everything you're reading. Your brain is judging my syntax, my writing style, whether or not this book is interesting, and perhaps even whether this book is worth finishing. And *all* of that is just your brain; *none* of that is The Real You. The Real You is the noticer of all of that stuff your brain is generating!

I know this is very counterintuitive, possibly confusing, and for some, rather out of the ordinary, so it may be uncomfortable and even a bit disturbing. That's OK. Those thoughts aren't The Real You either! The fact is that most people don't even think about this, because we're just not inherently wired this way. But once we're shown that there *is* a Real You that's doing the noticing, and we can learn to distinguish between The Real You and the never-ending stream of other stuff that your brain is generating, then you can distinguish The Real You that is doing the noticing! We can do this! All of us can do this! It just takes consistent practice and the will to step out of the old and into the new—a "new" that's always been there, but you perhaps didn't know was there.

So how do we learn to more clearly distinguish between brain-generated fluff and The Real You? What are some of the clues to tip us off that we're in our heads and not in our hearts? We'll cover those soon enough, but for now, please remember that your brain's job is to store information and pump out thoughts about what it has stored.

Your brain is like a hard drive. I don't know if you're familiar with how a hard drive works, but here's the layman's version, as this not-so-techie guy understands it. A hard drive has millions of little sectors that are either empty or filled with information, and each little sector has to have stuff dropped into it for us to be able to access that information in our computers. What I want you to do is to notice that your brain's job is to store something—anything that it can grab and store for later use—but it must have a place to store it, a very specific place.

Every thought, and every thought about the thought, is actually a very specific, distinct group of brain cells flashing together as your brain constantly separates, analyzes, sorts, and categorizes at almost-light-speed and with an ease that precludes our even noticing it. All of these little pieces of thought are dropped into the "memory bank," and stored for later use. We need our brains to remember things. That's one of your brain's primary jobs—to remember things. I know, I know, your brain does lots of other things—controlling the autonomic nervous system and other bodily functions like heartbeat, helping all of our organs to function in healthy unison, etc. I get all that, but for the purpose of this book, your brain's job is to store experiences for later use and to pump out those thoughts and thoughts about the thoughts as needed (whether or not you even want them at any given moment).

The more often you notice what your brain is generating, the more often you're standing in that noticer place, and the more often you're separating The Real You from this stuff being noticed. The more often you're noticing your brain moving one thousand miles per hour, the more you're grounding yourself in a place of stillness, watching your brain move one thousand miles per hour. The Real You is, when you're being the noticer, separate from all of this. The Real You is not your brain, it's the noticer of the brain. That is the you that's really you. You are not your brain. You're not even the body that has a brain in it. You're the noticer of the brain's thoughts. You're the noticer of the body's aches and pains, twitches, and everything else happening in there. The brain, when it's pumping out thoughts that you can notice, is just doing its job, which is to pump out those thoughts. The Real You's job is being noticer of the thoughts that your brain is generating.

The more you practice being the noticer, the more you'll be grounding yourself in that place of stillness and separating The Real You from your brain chatter.

Here's a tip, especially if you find this troubling at the moment, with all its newness and possible lack of familiarity: It's not about whether or not you get troubled or about if you "go there." It's about how long you *stay* there, and about who and how you're being once you catch "yourself" with The Real You, which is the noticer of all of that. The instant The Real You notices that the "you" in your brain is getting troubled, you are instantly separated from that which is generating the troubledness. If you

19

notice that you didn't catch yourself soon enough, or did it well enough, or thoroughly enough—none of which is The Real You—I recommend stepping back in the noticer place and offer up for your brain that judges some well-needed, likely long-overdue self-love and self-forgiveness. For those of you who don't know how or have forgotten how to apply that self-love and self-forgiveness, we'll cover self-love and self-forgiveness later in the book as well, just in case.

We have a myriad of problems to face every single day of our lives, and the more we look around, the more evidence of tension-causing situations there is to witness. Children, adolescents, and adults have pressure placed upon them daily by families and friends, schools, workplaces, and society in general. Making a living. Feeding our families. Caring for loved ones. Surviving the current or next global pandemic. Surviving global economic crisis. Ongoing wars and the threat of more wars every day around the world. Ongoing political, racial, religious, and assorted tensions in almost every nation on earth. Social justice issues to resolve. Battles over natural resources and financial resources. Increased costs on essential items like food, clothing, and housing. Families being broken apart and, even in those ever-more-rare homes when parents and their children stay together, parents are often having to work multiple jobs, which gives them even less time to instill cooperative values and loving ways of being into their children's hearts and minds.

We all wonder, "What am I supposed to do in the middle of all of this mess?!" A better question, and an important principle of The Real You, asks not, "What can I do with this?" but "Who can I *be* in the middle of all of this?!" Can you be the noticer of your brain going into frizzled-and-frazzled mode in the middle of the messiness? Remember, too, that this does not mean you are required to have control over your brain's ramblings or to come up with any solutions to the messiness. At least you're not required to have that brain-desired control that is generated by the brain's comparison of what's so vs. what you'd prefer (chatter vs. control of the chatter) until you've really grounded yourself in being the noticer. You're not even expected to have control over your feelings when they come up, because "feelings" are nothing more than a bodily reaction to the unreleased thoughts that you've allowed to simmer inside your brain to the point where corresponding brain chemicals got generated; and now those chemicals are floating around in your body, directly affecting it, often creating the future conditions of "dis-ease." Please understand that I know you may even find yourself getting "taken over" just by reading this book right now, which is not really "yourself," but is in fact the brain, which The Real You is not. Thoughts unreleased by the brain generate those chemicals that hit the body. Then, there may be a brain-body feedback loop that can sometimes feel like it's taking over. Your body reacts to the brain-generated chemicals caused by "your" (the brain's) thoughts running wild, and then your brain reacts to the body's reaction to the brain's reaction, and. . .you get the idea. The whole thing gets especially powerful when what your brain is noticing is something that means a lot to you. This leads to another of The Real You principles: *It always hurts exactly as much as you care that it be differently than what's so.* I'm not saying not to care, I'm saying this to remind you that if you find yourself upset over something, that you can, in fact, notice the upset and get under what's causing the upset. I'll get more into that shortly, but trust me, we will get to a process that can get you past the upset by stepping back from it and noticing it. Here's a short version.

Under anger is generally sadness that something happened that's made you angry.

Under the sadness about it is generally disappointment that something has happened that you didn't want to happen or something hasn't happened that you wanted to happen. This might be an unmet need, unmet preference, or unfulfilled expectation.

Under the disappointment—and the thing that always generates how big the disappointment is—is how much we care that things be different.

Under the caring is always *love*—love felt, love expressed, love gone missing, or love that's recognized as never having been there at all. But love is in all of it at some level. I don't want to get preachy here, but I have this expression,

Love is all there is.
All else we may perceive
is its absence.
- Brian Kurtz

The point is that you can, with practice (I hope you're not too tired of hearing me mention that), be the noticer of all that your brain is generating and all that your body is manifesting in response to what your brain is generating. When you truly ground yourself in the noticer place, you are separating The Real You from the brain, from the body, and even from all you may notice that is occurring around you.

If you're having a particularly challenging time getting back to peace by stepping back and being the noticer, that's OK. It takes practice like any new thing, right? We'll get to the "why" of why it takes a while; there's actually a process called "myelination" that needs to happen, but we'll get to that soon.

Meanwhile, here's an exercise that's guaranteed to chill you right out! Ready? Breathe in to a count of five and out to a count of eight. Do that four times. I know, it's just a book, but really, try it!

In to five. . ., out to eight . . .
In to five. . ., out to eight . . .
In to five. . ., out to eight . . .
In to five. . ., out to eight . . .

Pretty amazing, isn't it? What happens when we create a longer exhale after a shorter inhale is that this breathing protocol generates a relaxation response through the vagus nerve, which touches every major organ in your body. The longer exhale is generating an internal state that literally tells your body it's time to relax! Here's why I chose this count and this number of repetitions: when we stop a count on an odd number (five), there's a sort of unconscious need to continue the process. When we stop a count on an even number (eight), there's an unconscious recognition that the cycle has ended or has at least reached a state of "completion" even if it's not "finished." Repeating this short-inhale, long-exhale cycle four times (even number; could also be six times or eight times, if you find that many times necessary) completes the process psychologically.

If you need some clarification around the difference between "completion" and "finishing," consider a runner in a softball game. If the runner makes it to first, she hasn't made it all the way around to home plate, which would be finished, but having made it to first base is complete as far as safely reaching that segment of the base path is concerned. Stealing second base would be a completion as well, though still not finished. We can self-determine something to be complete when we've progressed to a given stage where we can acknowledge it as such. You will find that applying this principle to any complicated task makes it all much easier. Keep reaching stages of completion until the complex task is finished.

Here's another thing you can do when you're really triggered, upset, or just flat-out angry. It takes less time than the breathing exercise above, and is often every bit as effective.

Smile.

That's it. Smile. Try it. Now. Really.

No, not a half-baked half-smile, a really big smile. As big as you can make without hurting yourself. I'm watching you through the secret camera installed in the book . . . SMILE!

What happens when we smile a big smile is that we've catalyzed another "relaxation reboot" with the vagus nerve. Smiling a big smile, not just some halfway, fake, obligatory "say cheese for the camera" smile, when you're really not in the mood to do so, is not it. The coolest part is that even if you're faking it, this one still works!

Years ago I reached out to a friend because I'd not heard from her in what felt like years. She was kind of a "big wig" in the holistic community and was a real inspiration to me in so many ways. She was one of those always-grounded, peaceful, kind, soft-spoken Warrior Women who "walked her walk" with a calm determination that made her a natural leader, and beloved and appreciated by everyone who knew her.

I reached out and, much to my surprise, she said she'd been deeply depressed for several months, and that's why I hadn't heard from her. I offered to help her out and she said, "You don't understand. I'm literally chronically, clinically depressed and have been stuck here for months." I said, "*You* don't understand. I have a solution for your depression that I know will work. Let's get together for lunch, and I'll fix you right up!" She agreed to meet me in an hour or so at a diner midway between our homes, which were on opposite ends of town. But she warned me I was likely not going to succeed in lifting her out of her chasm.

I got there first and put my name on the list for a table for two in the more open area outside. She got there soon thereafter, before our table was ready, and we had a seat outside on a bench within earshot of the hostess so we'd hear my name being called.

I looked her in the eye, smiled, and asked, "How are you feeling at this very moment?"

"Horrible. As I told you I've been so deeply depressed nothing has helped."

"What would you do if I told you I can nail that depression in less than one minute?"

"I'd buy you lunch, for sure!"

"OK, Allie [not her name], ready?"

"For what?!"

"Smile."

"SMILE?! I don't FEEL LIKE SMILING! I'm FREAKING DEPRESSED!"

"Just force a big smile for me."

"ARE YOU PAYING ATTENTION?! I'm DEPRESSED! I DON'T FEEL LIKE SMILING!"

"Humor me. Just force a smile. A big one."

She gave me a half smile, as if that would shut me up, knowing it wouldn't.

"Come on, give me a big smile! Force a real smile, at least a real looking one, and make it a big one—for five measly seconds."

She did it. She gave me a really big smile and held that big smile for seven or eight seconds. . . . and lightly chuckled.

"See! See! Keep it going! How do you feel now?"

She laughed and smiled that big smile again.

"DAMN YOU! OK, I'LL BUY YOU LUNCH!"

It worked. She turned around several months of serious depression with a single smile . . . and we had a great lunch! Did she still have to deal with what was screaming loudly in her brain for all of those months? Yes, but she now knew that who she could be about it all had shifted.

I'm not saying anyone who's on medication for depression should ever go cold turkey off their doctor-prescribed medications. I'm also not saying that a single, longish smile can wipe away months of chronic depression. What I am saying is that a big smile is a very powerful thing that really works wonders in shifting the psycho-chemical brain processes that can do us both harm and good. Add the breathing exercise I mentioned earlier, and you have a powerful one-two punch that can knock out bad moods and even, at times, be a great first step toward easing or eliminating chronic depression.

Here's the thing: once you realize that you're not your brain, and you've realized that you *can* come to know both conceptually and in your heart and your gut (that Knowing which I promise will come later), that you really and truly are not your brain, and that you are, in fact, the noticer of it, you will come to know this Special Space as your own and not just a concept presented in this book. You will begin, with time and practice, to trust in this process and trust that just because some aspect of your life "has always been that way," it doesn't mean it has to stay that way. Just because a given life aspect has "never been that way," it doesn't mean it's not possible that it can be that way now. We'll get into greater depth with other processes in upcoming chapters. For now, know that this simple breathing exercise and/or a really big smile held for several seconds really does work well at turning your day around and maybe your life, if things have gone that far.

CHAPTER THREE

THE ATOM AND FINDING GOD

So now let's get to a less concrete but very important aspect of the process. We've asked, "Who is the 'I' who is noticing?" So now we may ask *where* is the "I" that you know exists, that's noticing the thoughts that your brain is generating?" I would assert that the noticer's location must be just outside the brain, where it can notice the brain generating the thoughts. To get a step closer to the answer, let's get scientific for a bit. If your brain wants to run away from science, notice that, and let it go!

Let's talk about atoms for a bit. Atoms are the building blocks of all known matter. They're very small, yet each of the elements in the periodic table is unique and wonderful in its own way. We could talk about platonic solids, the various colors on the table, and so forth, but that's for another book. Let's cover some of the basics that most never consider. There are protons and neutrons in a nucleus, surrounded by even-smaller orbiting electrons that are arranged in groups by distance known as "shells."

Everyone's seen the standard science class photo of an atom. What very few realize, however, is that this drawing we've all seen is not drawn to scale. If we were to magnify that atom out to a size in which the protons and neutrons were the size of glass marbles, the first shell-group of orbiting electrons would be ten miles away from the marbles in the nucleus! If that's not mind-blowing enough, the second shell of electrons would be as far away as the moon, some 250,000 miles—more than thirty earth-diameters—away from those marbles in the center. Astronomical distances indeed! The next shell would be at Jupiter, which is farther from us on Earth as the Earth is from the sun. Is your brain turning to jelly yet?

Here's the point: an atom is mostly empty space. It's so much mostly empty space it makes one wonder how we're even able to see each other (but that's another time and another book). Next point, there's an astounding amount of electromagnetic energy holding in place every piece of every atom. That energy is so powerful that, when harnessed, it can power a city, or if harnessed destructively, it can destroy a city. That's the amount of energy available in an atom. Everywhere. In everything.

I assert (free of any religious/evangelical connotations, I assure you!) that God/Spirit/Creator/Universe/Divine Consciousness is the source of that energy. If that is so, then we are literally made of mostly what I may as well call "godstuff." The godstuff that we are comprises what I'll call a soul. Some may call it consciousness. I'm talking about that "stuff" that Dr. David Hawkins called "our Eachness in the Allness." Wayne Dyer used the analogy of our bodies carrying "our bucket of the ocean." None of our buckets could ever contain the entirety of the ocean, yet each of our buckets contains the fullness and completeness of the *nature* of the ocean. As such, I believe that we all have access to that Infinite Divine Nature of which we are not just a part but to which we have ready access at the level of our own awareness. Not an awareness that we have, but the Awareness that we are. We are, literally, made mostly of that godstuff.

So if that energy is what holds our very subatomic particles together, and that godstuff is everywhere in everything in the known universe and beyond, then God/Creator therefore has nowhere to go because God is already everywhere in everything, right? So, God must, therefore, be operating in a place of *stillness*. Repeating yet again, when you're being the noticer of your brain moving a thousand miles an hour, you're placing The Real You into the stillness, watching your brain move a thousand miles an hour. The Real You—*in the stillness—is where your divinity lives!*

That Jesus guy is quoted as saying, "The kingdom of heaven lies within." Given this context, I'd have to agree with him. It's also without, as in everything.

Where is divine wisdom located? In the stillness where God is, to which we now all have full access. This is where the divine love is located. This is where that unconditional love, which is beyond brain-generated comparisons, brain-generated justifications for your or anyone's worthiness, may be found. Any other brain-generated hindrances to our having direct access to that place are thus rendered powerless! All of this beauty is always available in the stillness that we access by noticing what's not stillness. This is the place where peace lives. This is the place from which music and poetry and every type of expressed beauty within all of creation emanates.

There's a verse somewhere in the Judeo-Christian Bible that says something like, "Be still and know I am God." Noticing what is not stillness is how you place The Real You into that place where stillness simply is. Always. To access The Real You—and access all the wisdom and beauty available there—all you have to do is to be the noticer of whatever is there in your mind or in your body or in your outer world in order to be more fully present, free of judgments and comparisons and justifications and becauses that are likely always floating around in your brain while your brain is simply occupied being what it is and doing what it does.

Remember, too, that a key theme in this book is *not* that you need to frantically sort through what your brain thinks you must have and don't already have. It's about releasing what's in the way—those judgments, justifications, and becauses—that prevent us from just noticing and accessing all we already have living within us, and possibly even sourcing us, sourcing The Real You. They are all residing forever in the stillness to which the awareness that we are has consistently ready access.

In that ready access point are not necessarily all of the answers to life's deepest questions, but please notice that there's this Who or What inside of you that wants the answer to that question. I assert that this knower/seeker/desirer/distinguisher/classifier lives in your brain. I assert that the Knower lives within us all, and that your very physical reality—where the brain and body and life's occurrences exist here in the realm of 3D space and time—is all noticeable by The Real You. Once you've touched this place, you'll know that the part of you that requires control, order, familiarity, something to compare to something else, and above all else certainty—while quite necessary for us to function here in 3D—is not The Real You.

What I'm pointing to is that The Real You—the Noticer—is beyond time and space. And what of The Real You? When you die, the Real You—the Noticer—is what will be noticing you lying on the floor or hospital bed or wherever that may be at that transitory moment of time. It's there now, and it'll be there when your shell is no longer actively sourced by your Source Energy. Have a fear of death and dying? No need. The Noticer never dies and has no concerns of it. I've encountered people who don't even call that moment "death," referring to it instead as "making one's transition." John Lennon, in an interview shortly before his assassination, said "I don't fear death. It's just like getting out of one car and into another." Relax on that one. Nothing to fear.

More good news, and perhaps wonderful news for some: You do not need to calm your mind when you need only notice the brain's activity—even (and perhaps especially) when your brain is moving at speeds that defy time (like that dream that lasted for hours, but when you saw your clock it was only a few minutes later) that, if you tried to control that, might feel like more than you could ever handle. Yet when you watch that hypersonic activity, The Real You is in stillness watching your brain fly around at Mach 3!

Are you finding there's "too much" noise in there? What in you judges it to be too much? Your very noticing it (without letting it take you down the proverbial rabbit hole, please) immediately separates The Real You from the noise and places you in the stillness you're seeking!

We access that space by being the Noticer.

Because we generally identify with our brains' musings instead of with the noticer, we are often at the mercy of the brains' ideas, notions, perceptions, and declarations of reality, whether they're correct or not.

Don't get me wrong. I know we need our brains, but not for everything, and never for those moments in life that are most important: when it's time to trust in Knowing for yourself That Which Is Most You. When you come to a fork in the road on your way to your next appointment, you need your brain to help you know which way to turn.

When you come to a fork in the road of life, however, you need to tune into your heart/gut neural network.

"How do I do that?" your brain will likely ask.

The same way you access stillness.

"How do you access stillness?" your brain may ask.

By noticing what's not being still (noticing your brain growling, or your stomach growling).

How do you access silence? By noticing the seemingly never-ending noise. By being the noticer of it all.

Thanks to the Institute for Heart Math, that aforementioned organization that has for over thirty years researched the heart/gut neural network, we now know that the heart/gut neural network is actually sending more information to the brain than the brain is sending down to the heart/gut. This is becoming known in some scientific circles as "the second brain." More on that later.

On an old Gregg Braden podcast, he mentioned the existence of "sensory neurites," some 40,000 of them in the heart/gut neural network that may assist in providing that Knowing and make available that certainty, that "knowing that you know that you know." Think for a moment about how tiny 40,000 cells are in a body of 30,000,000,000 (that's thirty *billion*) cells. Yet somehow these provide access to the Divine Knowledge that can come "through you as you" for yourself and everyone you will touch in your life. Apparently, we don't need much of "the good stuff" for it to make an impact.

Spend as much conscious, willful, intentional time in the noticer place as you can each day. The more time you spend there, the more refined your sense of reality will become. The more time you spend there, the more oriented to accessing that place you'll become and the easier it will be to access it, not by "trying" to get there, but by simply being there once you get centered in what that feels like. The more time you spend there, the sooner you can catch yourself when you've not been being there, thus making it easier to reconnect to that place as you pull yourself out of any psychological/emotional hole into which you may have momentarily fallen. Now, instead of falling down into that seemingly bottomless rabbit hole of depression, despair, confusion, frustration, anger, sadness, disappointment and pain, *you can catch yourself just by being the noticer of it all,* and the instant you do catch yourself and realize that who and what you really are is the noticer, there is, and need never again be, any concern about that rabbit hole. No more climbing and clawing! In the very moment of awareness with the Awareness that you are—read that again . . . not an awareness that you come to and thus have, *with the awareness that you are*—everything in your life changes. That Real You place is always available, and the teaching, learning perspective you're reading about now will place you there anytime you're able to remember this simple-not-easy essential truth.

Here's your homework forever: Notice the thoughts your brain is generating but possibly in a way unlike any of your previous noticing.

Notice your thoughts like you'd notice cars driving by as you're standing on the corner (safely on the corner; I'm not asking you to step out into traffic!) alongside a busy freeway intersection. Notice your thoughts like the cars driving by—there goes a blue Ford, a red Pontiac, a black Toyota, a gold Mercedes-Benz—not, "Wow! Look at that exquisite sedan!" Not a great car or a lousy car, nor judging that they're going too slow or too fast, or that there are too many or too few cars, or any judgment or valuation of them . . . just notice them and let them go by. Notice your thoughts in this manner. Just notice and release the thoughts without any thoughts about the thoughts.

Now notice that while you're standing still, safely on the street corner, while thousands of cars are racing by, you can notice your thoughts in this manner. Let them come and go. Let them arise and let them fall away. More come up, and you let them fall away.

This is your homework forever.

Why is this homework so important? Remember that thoughts are brain cells flashing together in a specific combination. A thought about the thought is a combination of some of those brain cells combined with others, and so on. If we don't willfully, intentionally release the thought, after about twenty seconds, the brain begins to generate a chemical corresponding to the thought! Soon we have happy chemicals, sad chemicals, disappointed or angry chemicals, frustrated chemicals floating around in our brains, and soon there's a result of these chemicals when this biochemistry hits our bodies. The bodily reaction to the thought is often what we perceive as emotions—the physical response to the thought. If we're not careful, fear thoughts can creep in, resulting in a bodily "fight or flight or freeze" response, and soon we're in big trouble and can get trapped in that feedback loop mentioned earlier. The more time we spend there, the more we're at the mercy of our brain chatter, and the more that stuff takes up residence in our bodies as dis-ease! This is why we must let that stuff go! We must not allow our brain chatter to destroy us, to destroy our most cherished relationships, and to destroy the world we so tenuously share.

CHAPTER FOUR

POINT A AND POINT B

As we notice our thoughts, releasing them on their way, and eventually not even holding them at all, allowing them to flow by like cars on the expressway, we will soon notice that *there are issues* that are continuously arising in our brains throughout our day. Ready to begin breaking those down for study, processing, and elimination? Let's start here.

Here's the next Real You principle: *All issues have what I call a "Point A" and a "Point B," where Point A is what is objectively so about a person, place, situation, or condition, and Point B is what we'd prefer instead of Point A!*

"He said x (Point A), but I wish he'd said y (Point B)."

"She did x (Point A), but I wish she'd have done y (Point B)."

"I have $1000 in my bank account (Point A), but I wish I had $5000 in my bank account (Point B)."

"I have $1,000,000 in my bank account (Point A) and I wish I had $2,000,000 in my bank account (Point B)."

"My nose (pick any body part) is big/small/crooked/asymmetrical (Point A), and I wish it was (anything but that, right?) (Point B)"

"I feel x right now (Point A)," and I sure wish I felt y instead (Point B)."

The list could go on forever regarding your brain-generated preferences, right? The really sick-and-possibly-twisted part about all of this is that even if you have tons of money, for example, your brain will want more. If you're a great looking guy, you may still pick some body part, height, weight, etc., that you'd prefer instead. If you've read any of Brené Brown's books, you already know that women have the hardest time of all, where any part of any body part is subject to inner and outer criticism, none of which is coming from The Real You.

Someone you care about may say something you wish they'd said differently or not said at all. Your favorite sports team might win a game, but you wish they'd won by a wider margin, perhaps to win a bet, or just because you really wanted them to not just win but put an epic beat-down on a heated rival. It could be anything! Even if something makes you happy, if it's a *conditional* happiness, that is, based on something happening a certain way at a certain time, when that condition is no longer being met, that change will cause some degree of upset just because it's not exactly as we'd prefer. Every issue you can ever name has a Point A, that which is so about the person, circumstance, or condition, and a Point B, which you'd prefer instead of Point A. There are no exceptions to this. Not happy about that? NOTICE THAT!

This brings us to the next Real You principle: *If there's an issue, there will always be a distance between Point A and Point B—this distance is the very definition of duality consciousness!* The "distance" could be how far off the "what's so" is compared to "what you'd prefer" instead. The distance could be how much money you have compared to how much you'd prefer, or what a dear friend said compared to what you'd prefer he or she had said, even if they'd complimented you to a new potential date you've been eyeing, maybe they didn't say it in quite the way you'd prefer they'd said it. Any and all issues have this distance aspect. This could even be time related. Here's an example.

I'm on a road trip promoting my book, and I let you know I'm coming in to see you for a scheduled cup of coffee at, say, 3 p.m., before I have my evening dinner and presentation. You're waiting for me, and I don't show up until 3:05 p.m. You know I'm coming from afar, so when I'm not there at 3:00, or 3:03, or 3:04, it's not that big a deal. I show up five minutes late. It's only five minutes late, and you know I'm never very late, so it's not a big deal.

Now, consider that same five minutes when I'm due and not yet present at your perfectly prepared wedding venue, and you've asked me to marry your daughter to your future son-in-law! Now how are you feeling? It's their wedding, so it's VERY MUCH A BIG DEAL, RIGHT?! Notice that it's the same five-minute difference as being a little late for our coffee date, but *how much you care about that difference makes all the difference!*

After realizing that every issue has a Point A and a Point B, we can take the next step of self-examination and self-education.

You've noticed there's always a Point A (what's so) and a Point B (what you'd prefer instead). Imagine these are toothpicks, and imagine dropping "Toothpick A" and "Toothpick B" into a "bowl of awareness." As we peer into the bowl of awareness, we notice the toothpicks have come together at the bottom of the bowl. Here is the place where we may ask ourselves, in the awareness of any charge, any upset, any preferences that are not being met, any needs unmet, or any expectations unfulfilled, "Why is this Point B an issue for me? Why is it a preference for me? Why is it important to me?"

Remember that the noticing is itself the access point to the awareness that you are. In that awareness you can not only notice that there is an unmet preference or an unfulfilled expectation, you can also (very important) notice who you're being about the person, place, thing, condition, or situation in which you find yourself at that moment. The wedding example above is an obvious one, but perhaps your motivation is more subtle. Perhaps a physical characteristic—my nose, for example—is an issue. My nose was broken multiple times as a too-short, middle-school point guard trying to get a rebound, who got elbowed in the nose as part of the rebounder's clear-out move. There are, even now, times when my brain chatter reminds me that some may find my right-pointing proboscis to be a curiosity or even a conversation starter ("Dude! What's up with that thing on your face?!"), or just downright unattractive to people who prefer cute little turned-up button noses, or perfectly symmetrical noses, or whatever. My preference is that I be attractive as opposed to being unattractive.

My preference is that I'm not perceived as some strange-looking guy with a big thing on his face. My preference is that when I'm doing a speaking engagement that people are focused on what I'm saying and not on my nose!

Remember that none of this need even exist in reality, at least for the most part, except when the derogatory self-torment is alive and well, usually treating me not so well, amid the never-ending stream of stuff that characterizes my brain chatter.

So, what can you do about this never-ending brain chatter?

You can notice it, which instantly separates The Real You from it! You need not go down the rabbit hole your brain wants you to follow. You can and must, however, notice that inherent in every issue you will ever notice, in every upset you will ever notice, and in everyone and anything that causes you any disturbance whatsoever, there is always a Point A and a Point B. As soon as you can notice the upset/issue taking place, please step back and notice not only that there *is* a Point A and a Point B, but also ask yourself "What makes that Point B BE a Point B for me in the first place?" What is the comparison between what's so and the unmet preference? What is the comparison between what's so and the unfulfilled expectation?" What is the value judgment you're holding on to about yourself, the situation, etc. based on? What is it that you're noticing that has triggered you into a reaction instead of a measured, awareness-based response? What do you really want instead of what you're experiencing, having, feeling, or dealing with?

Here's another crucial piece of information, and it may shake up your entire existence until now. Ready? Take a few deep breaths before continuing. Breath in to five and out to eight, four times. Do this before continuing. Really. I know it's a book. Do it, OK?? Go!

In . . ., out . . .

Cool air in. . . .warm air out.

Notice you're inhaling when you're inhaling, and notice you're exhaling when you're exhaling.

In . . ., out . .

How's that feel? Better? More relaxed? More present?

Here's a practical point from a somewhat metaphysical viewpoint. If we are cocreators with Creator, and if our thoughts can become reality, then worry is asking for what we don't want! But what do we do when we have a natural tendency to worry, which is, for the record, always grounded in a history-based point of view, which is, by definition, brain-generated? We must separate consciously and intentionally Our Real Selves from our brain chatter. We are not our brains, nor are we the body that has a brain in it that is generating the thoughts we are noticing. We are the noticers of our brain chatter, and the way we access that magical place of peace amid the brain chatter, nervous stomach, and sense of overwhelm about the world around us is by being the noticer of it all. In the awareness of that noticing, we negate the charge around the thought and ground ourselves in the place where that awareness lives in us. In that moment, you know you are standing in the place of The Real You.

"How do we get out of the mess where our brains have so often planted us?"

By noticing it all and by practicing the practical and easy steps mentioned a few pages ago. If we can be the noticer of the crazed, frantic, and powerful thoughts, and remember that they are nothing more than thoughts generated by our brains, and that we are not our brains but the noticer of them, we can, in being the awareness that we are, release the thoughts, negate the charge carried by the thought, and recenter ourselves back in to the stillness of the noticer place. Regardless of the sheer volume and volume level of the brain chatter, we can, with some practice, work our way back to peace, even in the midst of what might otherwise appear to be enormous upset and trauma.

There's more good news, in case your brain is now trying to come up with ways to dispute the effectiveness of the process just mentioned! Even if we're a little late in catching it, and the brain and body have already started that possibly overwhelming feedback loop between the body reacting to the brain and the brain then reacting to the bodily reaction, we still can, as The Noticer, ease the whole process back toward calm by noticing our bodily reaction and noticing the thoughts, which become possible when we remember we are not our brains, or even the body, or even the circumstances about which our brains have issues. We are the noticers of our brains and bodies and circumstances.

Here's the next piece about issues in general: we all have *attachments* to those thoughts that our brains are generating. Notice that! We want our thoughts to be the best, most well-considered thoughts. We want our thoughts to be the most correct, justifiable, right, righteous, and most perfect thoughts because we thought of them! Ever notice a four-year-old who proudly comes up and does this exact same thing? Or when the young child thinks he's outsmarted you because he's come up with what feels like a really original plan or deception to trick you into something he wants you to do? Yep, parts of you are still like that little mischief maker.

There are things about your life about which you may not be totally happy. Perhaps they've become irritating on some level, in a small or perhaps a large way; no matter how you may want to reframe them, avoid them, slap some pretty paint on them with the coping mechanisms and defense mechanisms and suppressions and denials we all generate at times, they're not what you'd otherwise prefer.

Here's the most important piece of information, a foundational Real You Principle, and the one that helped me get past the twenty-plus years of abuse I took growing up: *It's never been about what happened to you, it's always been about who you've been being about it.* Who we're being about it is exactly the reason why our Point B is a Point B! So, what's hidden in the Point B? When we stop and notice there is a Point B and get under it, we can do some self-study and learn more about who we are and how we operate, and we can learn more about what our preferences are and why, and work on that!

Why is this important? Like that hard drive, our brains must, to function, separate, divide, sort, analyze, and characterize so they can store it for later! The catch, of course, is that the brain does that with everything, and that activity is usually running the show until we notice that's what's happening! As soon as we can notice this occurring, we're instantly out of the stuckness, anger, frustration, disappointment, pain, angst, etc. just by being The Noticer.

Now, of course, there will be something that becomes quite obvious rather quickly as you become a more proficient noticer. You'll notice all of your life's issues! As you may now be noticing all of the issues that have Point As and Point Bs, trust that this is not a new thing. In fact, thousands of years ago, the men who wrote the Old Testament (I assume they're men because the now almost 6,000-year-old Hebrew writings are distinctly patriarchal) used the very first story after the description of creation as a perfect teaching moment. And most everyone misses it. In fact, I believe clergy has for thousands of years deliberately and consistently deluded congregants of synagogues and churches from its true meaning as a vehicle of control over you. I'm speaking about the Adam and Eve story.

CHAPTER FIVE

THE REAL STORY OF ADAM AND EVE

This chapter may get my book banned, but I'll take my chances. If you're a member of an Abrahamic faith, do you remember the message so many were taught? Original Sin, that is, Adam and Eve disobeying God, failing to follow the one simple rule with which they were charged, was due to an inherent human flaw. It is written that God gave Adam and Eve everything and they blew it. Before I continue, know that you can skip down several paragraphs if you find the whole story as demeaning and aggravating as I do, and you can get to my version of the Adam and Eve story and how I view the real message the original writers intended.

Clergy have for centuries taught that we as a human species—as direct descendants of Adam and Eve—had it all and blew it. Because Adam and Eve blew it, we are thus guilty by association, and we're told that their error was not even by choice! We've been told that there must be something inherently wrong with Adam and Eve, and thus also with us that is uncorrectable on our own, thus requiring:

- Strict adherence to the 613 rules of The Law in the Old Testament, which, then and now, are pretty much impossible to follow, and

- Strict adherence to the principles described in the New Testament, most of which are not even attributed to Jesus but to writings by the apostle Paul, who wrote letters to congregations he'd helped organize and establish. These letters were determined to not be just mail sent by a caring leader to his "flock," but have come to be considered immutable laws to be followed as if they'd been written by God Himself. (Notice the *Him* in himself, since we're talking about a patriarchy after all, and the penalty for failing to do so as declared, we're told, by an all-knowing and all-loving God is *eternal* hellfire and damnation?! WHAAAAT?!

Again, the need for these writings goes far beyond just helping define more clearly for us rules governing every segment of our lives. There's an underlying message, as interpreted by clergy and some Christian scholars, that we must have these rules, because we could never live a life worth living without these rules, because we're all living in an imperfect and "fallen" state. Because the rules are pretty much impossible to follow anyway, we are, in advance of our even being born, said to be in need of a redeemer. Because they say we're inherently flawed, we need someone or something to give us the rubber stamp of acceptability when we die, so that we can get into a place reserved only for those people wearing that stamped badge of honor. Those who lack the holy seal of approval are rejected out of hand, and we've heard where those folks go, right?!

Now, of course, since they say no one can possibly live up to these standards, we need some sort of redeemer. Anyone who's ever lived—in such an inherently flawed existence—is and was in trouble from the moment of creation, according to them, thus we are pretty much expected to carry guilt over our flawed actions. But even this self-imposed guilt trip is insufficient by that mandatory belief system. We must be reminded that there is something *in* us, *about* us, that *is* us that's flawed, and is therefore worthy of constant and lifelong *shame,* the lowest of the low vibrational states of being.

Those wishing to "guide" us planted and nurtured this seed of self-insufficiency. Do we, in this viewpoint, have any chance whatsoever to survive the here and now, much less to live on happily and joyfully into eternity? Not within this trap. We were locked into that dogmatic predicament from the moment that snake (just to make the story more interesting) convinced Eve (patriarchy, remember? it's always the woman's fault) to convince Adam (males who err are victims, but still somehow worthy of ruling the family, congregational units, and the world) to eat that fruit, and humanity has been rotten to the apple core ever since.

OR NOT!

Here's my take on the Adam and Eve story; similar, but with a much happier ending! Ready? Here goes.

God creates the Garden of Eden, then creates Adam and Eve, the snake, and everything else in the garden. Then it's time for The Talk.

"Hey, Adam and Eve! I'm God. I created you and everything you see here. The weather is so perfect here in the Garden, you don't even need to wear clothes. The ground here is so soft, you don't even need a bed to rest and sleep on. Everything here is perfect, and because I love you so much, I've created it just for you! You will love it here! All I want you to do is just be here, be fruitful, and multiply. That's all. Just *be*. Oh, yeah! I've given you some super-sensitive body parts that will make it really enjoyable when you're being fruitful and multiplying. You're going to LOVE being fruitful and multiplying. You're going to want to do it all day! I love you! Enjoy!"

Then, of course, God continued, "Almost everything here in the Garden is all yours. There is one catch, however. See that tree over there (illuminating The Tree containing the Knowledge of Good and Evil to make sure they see it clearly)? *DO NOT EAT THE FRUIT FROM THAT TREE. AVOID THAT TREE AT ALL COSTS! I DO NOT WANT YOU TO HAVE THE KNOWLEDGE OF GOOD AND EVIL. STAY AWAY FROM THAT TREE! I WARN YOU TWO, STAY AWAY FROM THAT TREE! All else here is yours. Just stay away from that tree, OK?*"

Well, we know what happened next. Eve was approached by a snake (it had to be some creature that scares some folks, creeps around on the ground, etc.; let's face it, a cute talking parrot or smiling puppy would never work, right?) that convinced her (patriarchal writers, remember? so it had to be the woman's fault) to convince Adam (the man had to be the victim, due to the patriarchal culture of the writers) to eat some of that fruit.

Adam ate some of the fruit and suddenly was bestowed with the knowledge of *good and evil*. He then gives some to Eve, and suddenly she too has the knowledge of good and evil. Now they both have the knowledge of good and evil. They then look down at their bodies and realize, "We're not wearing any clothes! Is that good or evil? It must be evil, so we'd better cover ourselves!" Fig leaves are immediately grabbed and placed over their bodies, especially those supersensitive body parts, and they begin to relax a bit until they realize and exclaim, "Oh no! We disobeyed God after God gave us this perfect place made just for us, and these oh-so-pleasureful body parts to encourage us to be fruitful and multiply! We're in BIG trouble now!" At that point, they run and hide in the bushes, and God pops back in (because God is God, after all, and sees the whole thing happen) and asks, "So hey, Adam and Eve, my beloved children, how's the first ten minutes in the garden been going?"

Can't you just hear Adam and Eve?!

"Well, there was this snake, and she's stupid and gullible and weak, and she convinced me to try some of the fruit. And I was stupid and gullible and weak, and they made me try some, and we feel so guilty and ashamed! Whatever can we do now, God!?"

Let's now take a look at the Adam and Eve story from a stepped-back perspective. The knowledge of good and evil is, by definition, an "either/or." What God was saying, by my version of the story, is that "the knowledge of good and evil" represents *dualistic thinking*. All God wanted from Adam and Eve was to *just be* in the Garden of Eden. Just be fruitful and multiply. Instead of just *being* there (Ram Das would certainly approve of Be Here Now, right?!), they chose to operate from a dualism symbolized by the Tree of the Knowledge of . . . you guessed it . . . good and evil.

What this means, by my interpretation of the Adam and Eve story, is that instead of operating from a heart-centered unity consciousness (be here now), they chose to operate in a dualistic way of being, which is the way our *brains* operate and not our hearts. The whole point of the Adam and Eve story was to *let our hearts run our lives and not our brains* and to operate in unity consciousness, not duality consciousness.

So what's the real point of presenting this other interpretation of the Adam and Eve story? Beyond the requisite victimization, guilt, and shame, the actual possibility on a moment-by-moment basis is that we can, from of The Real You place, begin to realize (as in "to make real" and generate a level of awareness of and for yourself) that there are obstacles to Divine Connection, and all of these obstacles may be worked with, processed through, and evolved beyond. If we can touch that divine place to which The Real You is inexorably connected, and stay there as required until we are deeply rooted in The Real You way of being, we're home free. And since The Real You is the place where our divinity resides, we've always had ready access; it's been a simple-but-not-easy matter of *awareness* that we have *always* been home free!

Remember, the brain's job is to store information for later use, and the way it stores information is by separating everything from everything else. Original sin was not disobeying God. Original sin was never about disobeying God and was never about some inherent flaw in human nature that required we be redeemed, saved, or somehow changed. Original sin was *letting the brain run the show, and our identifying ourselves with that and not with our inherent divinity,* which is the place from which flows peace, love, poetry, music, and all that's ever been worthwhile in human existence.

Adam's eating the fruit which gave him the knowledge of good and evil implies to me that the ancient writers of this story understood that the brain's job is to separate everything from everything else so it can be stored for later. The problem with that is that the brain is, if we let it run the show, operating in a manner that is inherently flawed, because then everything is separated from everything else, which is then separating us from God, from each other, and from our own divine nature. When we step into the noticer place, we're stepping out of the brain's required duality consciousness and into our true reality as divinely-sourced, Spirit-filled fleshbags operating in unity consciousness, One with All That Is.

47

Here's another Real You principle: *Any time you can notice a comparison and contrast, you've been in duality-grounded, brain-generated error, and in an awareness separate from the Awareness that you are—The Real You.* Any time you can notice good/evil, right/wrong, you/me, or division by nationality, religion, skin color, or your favorite sports team, you're not in The Real You place where all of The Good Stuff lives.

How do we stop getting sucked in and dragged down, exhausted by, and worn out by our brain chatter? We can stop and notice it and begin in that moment to step back from it, operating from the inherently healthier guidance of the heart/gut neural network and not from the flawed brain-centered guidance. Counterintuitively, once again, the way to extricate yourself from the brain chatter trap and to ground yourself in this inherently beautiful Beingness is by simply noticing the brain chatter.

Any judgment, evaluation, determination of worth or lack thereof, any value attached to anything—"I'm a good person," or "I'm a terrible person," or "What's wrong with him?!" or "It's so obvious that politician is a crook!" or "That politician is a wonderful leader and someone I totally trust!" are all comparisons of one thing to another, of one aspect of something to another, of a preference unmet or expectation unfulfilled. All are comparisons comparable to the Point A/Point B referenced earlier. Any time there's a distance between Point A and Point B, this distance defines duality consciousness and *defines all suffering on some level.* And remember that other Real You principle—the intensity of the suffering is always exactly as much as you wish it to be different than it is!

Now, let's get to a process that works wonders with all of those Point Bs you've been noticing. I call it "Resolve-Refine-Release."

CHAPTER SIX

RESOLVE

There are three ways to be about any issue once you've noticed that there is one. First, you can work to *resolve* the issue. If you've done all you can to resolve it and it simply won't resolve, which does happen from time to time, the next step is to work on *refining* who you're going to be about that thing you can't resolve. If you've done all the refining you can do and there's still more that remains, there's only one thing left to do and that's to *release* what's left. That last part—release—is the simplest and hardest one to apply in our task-oriented, results-oriented Western culture, but we will nail that one down, too!

Please remember that these three ways of being require that you do them in order! If you slide past trying to resolve the issue and work on refining who you're going to be about it, you've not actually done the work required, both internally and externally. You may find that what you're calling "refinement" at that point will often end up being just a conglomeration of compensatory thought-mechanisms and coping behaviors you've developed to avoid, deny, or suppress the issue at hand and not actually resolve it. Likewise, if you bypass resolving and refining and just work on releasing, you'll soon find there's just too much mess to deal with by simply tossing it away and that it keeps coming up for resolution anyway. You must do all of your inner work to get there!

Let's first cover *resolve*. Before setting out to resolve any issue, perspective is a key component. Einstein said something to the effect of "the mindset that created the problem will not be the mindset that provides the solution." Remember Point A and Point B? Let's start with where we are (Point A, what's actually so) and compare that to where we want to be (Point B). "I have $1000 in my checking account (Point A), and I'd surely prefer to have $5000 in my checking account (Point B)!" Or perhaps "My wife keeps saying I'm not paying enough attention to her (Point A). I wish she'd be happier with the time we spend talking, and I know that I need to be paying more attention to her in the way she can see that!" (Point B).

Or maybe your Point A is, "He said I should let my hair grow longer," and Point B might be "I wish he was happy with my hair the way it is, because it's a hassle taking care of long hair."

Perspective around the situation becomes crucial here. It starts with noticing there is an issue (bank account total or appreciation for quality time or length of hair) and that any issue is based on a comparison between what's so about the situation (Point A), and what you'd prefer (Point B) instead of Point A!

Step One in the resolving process is "zooming out" and taking a healthy and introspective look at where you are, as well as at the goal/end point; that is, where you want to be and what that result looks like, how it feels, who's there with you as you get to that point, and any other details about what that may look like. By "healthy," I mean looking at where you are, what you've been doing, and who you've been being that's brought you to this point with regard to the issue at hand, with a self-loving, self-forgiving, and constructively critical eye—not with the typically human eye for self-deprecation, history-based hopelessness, or other self-defeating attitude that will prevent you from seeing your present situation with a clearer filter. Noticing what your brain is doing at this moment is crucial to bringing a more objective awareness to the situation. Again, remember that it's not about stopping your brain! It's about simply noticing it, letting those thoughts roll on by like cars on the expressway and, after identifying any "Point Bs," allowing them up for exploration and learning.

Once you get a vision or idea of how that end result might appear, look at what's along the path from "now" to "then" and consider objectively what obstacles, duties, or other aspects are required to be completed, navigated, or otherwise handled to get you from "here" to "there." Notice, I'm separating "now" from "then" and "here" from "there." Notice as well that I've not mentioned anything about these obstacles being hard/easy, quick/time-consuming, or other dualistic judgments about them.

It's important to remember, too, that everything from your past happened in a "now" moment then, and anything you're seeking in your future will happen in a "now" moment then. All we ever really have is *now,* so be present to every step along the path toward the resolution of the issue at hand.

There's a Bible verse about this (again, no religion here, just presenting a valid symbolic point) that says, "Lord, be a Lamp unto my feet." You may have heard the expression, but few, I've learned, are familiar with the context around where the verse originated.

Back in the days of the nomadic Hebrews roaming the desert, the summers were so brutally hot that they erected tents during the day to block the sun's rays, thus cooling the sand enough for them to survive until nightfall, when they'd pack up their tents and belongings and do their travelling.

They'd look up to the stars—that is, symbolically, to God in Heaven above—using them to navigate their general direction. It was, however, quite dark in the desert, so the wanderers made shoes with up-turned toe-tips on which they'd place candles to light a small portion of the ground around them. With these "lamps" on their shoes, they could see just enough to make a safe "next step." These "lamps" were literally as well as symbolically lighting their way in the darkness. "Lord, be a lamp unto my feet" was thus their way of saying "God, please just show me the next specific and correct step to take in the here and now, and I'll keep my focus on you regarding the general direction and path toward the future outcome I'm seeking."

If you're attuned to a general direction or task orientation or life-path, what remains once you're in that "groove" is to keep your eyes open! Be the noticer of what's occurring in your brain about the subject about which you're trying to work toward resolution. Be present to any feelings in your body that might clue you in to triggers or upsets or excitements. Notice as well what's occurring around you that may be God/Spirit/Universe showing you through a synchronicity moment what that next right step might be! Keep your eyes, ears, and heart open to receiving the next bit of intuitively-provided instructions in whatever way they may be shown to you, and trust the answer when it really and truly feels like something "you know that you know." I get "red lights" of instantly feeling like the glands in my neck are swelling, or a sudden slight pain in my gut or lower back or knees. I get "green lights" when the hair on my arms or on the back of my neck stand up.

Noticing your attitude is crucial during this "zoom out" to see what your path toward resolution looks like. Any concerns or worries about possible future disappointment are nothing more than brain-generated fluff; often no more than an unfounded future grounded in a brain-remembered past and not even focused on the present shown by that "lamp unto your feet." At some point, this past-remembering, future-concerned caution may have served you as a way to manage risk and danger but may now have become nothing more than fear-based distractions that, once again, prevents you from being in the now-moment available to you.

One more huge point with regard to progress toward resolving any issue is that you have trust and faith in yourself and, if you're willing, it may well serve you to consider that there might actually be a higher power in and around you that may actually be supporting you along your way. Remember that you are literally made of godstuff, so it's not like you have to look elsewhere for that divinely-inspired Source of information. It's already in you and all around you!

The more clearly you can notice what's happening in your brain, in your body, and in the world around you, the more firmly you can stand in that place of Awareness of it all, watching with eager anticipation all that's happening; awaiting the next "bread crumb on the path," to choose an analogy from the old children's story of Hansel and Gretel. When you're in a place of faith and trust that it's all going your way (pronoia, as opposed to paranoia), even when it doesn't look at the moment that things are going your way, then what look like obstacles can now become teaching tools to get you past them to what's next along your path toward resolution.

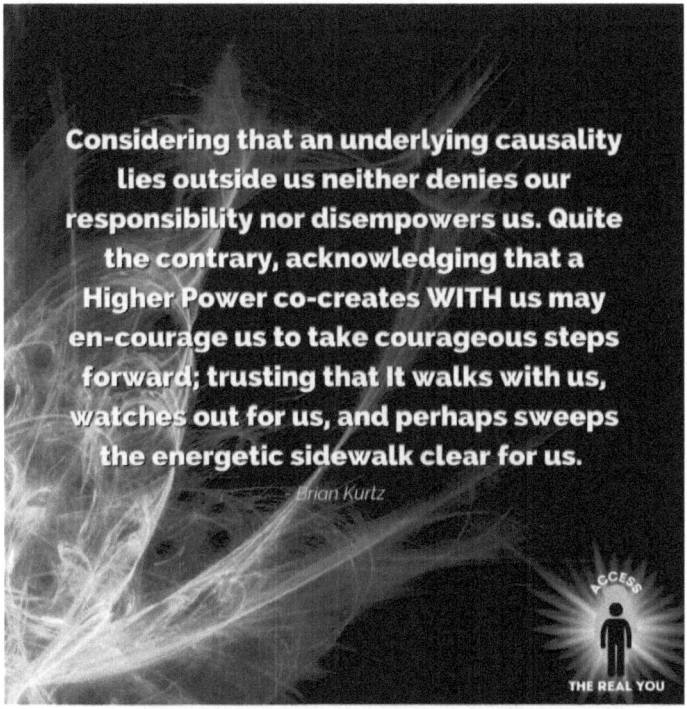

Considering that an underlying causality lies outside us neither denies our responsibility nor disempowers us. Quite the contrary, acknowledging that a Higher Power co-creates WITH us may en-courage us to take courageous steps forward; trusting that It walks with us, watches out for us, and perhaps sweeps the energetic sidewalk clear for us.

Brian Kurtz

Think of where you are now and go back to some really challenging circumstances in your past. If you have done your work about and around these items, you have learned something from them, right? Approach your history with reverence and thanks for what it has taught you, and do not carry the burdensome anger, grief, regret, or other feelings that may have accompanied the struggle at the time. Approach your future with eyes wide open, expecting the next wonderful thing that's about to happen. Might it also be challenging? Sure, but don't drop into "struggle mode" before you get there. Hold on to a more constructive attitude of confidence, trusting in yourself as you walk along in the possibly uncertain moments along the way. Approach your present moment with at worst (Eckhart Tolle recommends these three): a level of acceptance, or up from there enjoyment, and at best, enthusiasm!

Let's talk a bit about that acceptance piece. Acceptance is inherently neutral, and it's always easier to work from a situation that's neutral and work toward a positive than it is to work from a negative to a neutral and then finally to a positive.

Ever heard someone say dejectedly about a situation that "It is what it is?"

If it really is "what it is," that's a neutral! The person, condition, or circumstance simply "is what it is." If, however, we're just being sarcastic, hopeless, and operating from a place of resignation, we're not being neutral, we're actually becoming a negative perspective. You've likely heard, "What we perceive we receive," or, "You'll get what you expect."

Another Real You principle is centered around "holding space."

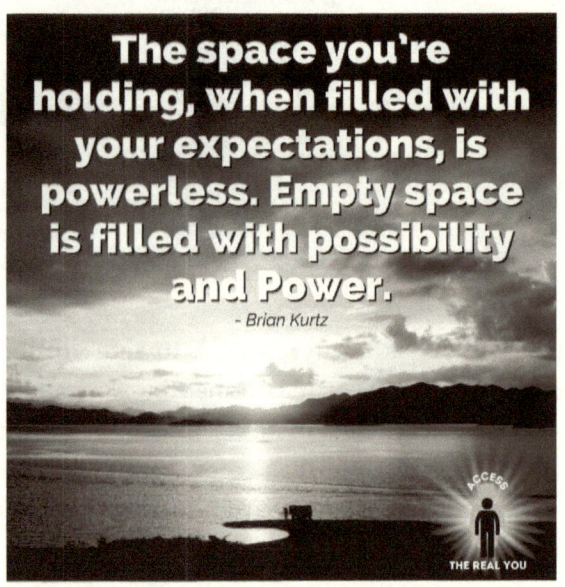

Remember that God/Source/Creator is in the empty spaces? The space you're holding, when you're messing it up, is always filled with your expectations, so be careful about your expectations, as well as about your perceptions of what's happening around you. If we're holding inherently neutral and empty Sacred Space, the only thing in there is a loving divinity. If we're dropping our hopes and preferences into the space, we're not giving God/Spirit/Creator a chance to show up there with our Best and Highest solution. Make sure the space you're holding is freed from your preferences, desires, and expectations!

If you're holding space and trusting in Spirit to guide you in a general direction, purpose, and path, you can watch with eager anticipation what's in front of you. If you know you're on the right path, then any apparent or perceived obstacle is just another thing to go *through* to get *to* where you're headed! If what you've done looks like a mistake, cut yourself some slack! Love yourself! Forgive yourself! It's just another step of guidance, tipping you back in the right direction! If you keep seeing something better on the horizon, don't beat yourself up about not getting there yet. Remember that you've gotten this far so that you can see what's out there on the horizon! Self-love and self-forgiveness are the key elements here. If you can stand in this place, you can realize that nothing has ever happened *to* you, and everything that has gotten you to here and now (as in reading this book) is happening *for* you.

Are you noticing your imperfections or "what's still missing" that you need to succeed? The very fact that you can see what's missing, or where you're not as yet, proves that you're seeing that which is more of what you're seeking! Work toward that place!

If you're not where you want to be, check your bearings. Is it progress or are you farther off target? Are you on track or farther off center? If a course correction, attitude adjustment, or just a little rest is in order, cut yourself some slack and keep walking from there! I've often found that the harder I try, usually coming from an energy of lack, I notice a charge that might give me more of that "type-A" drive, diligence, and task-oriented fervor, but I've found that way of being inherently stressful. If you're envisioning with self-trust, self-love, and self-forgiveness seeing a successful moment in a future time, feel into that and keep walking, keeping your mental "space" empty and allowing into that space only that which serves. Do likewise by noticing what's occurring around you. If you're walking your walk with a mind free of lack, and fear, and, specifically, brain-derived preferences, you may be too busy looking for what you expect and not what might be exactly what you most need, which may not look as you'd expect at all and is already in and all around you, awaiting your discovery in the synchronicity of it all!

If you're "going through hell" keep walking! Notice and keep going from there! You may still have your stuff about it. It may not be "fun" at all, but in the noticing, you can have your stuff and not allow it to have you!

When you zoom out to a higher place and do some self-examination of your preferences and your "Point B's," you're doing some really valuable work! The deeper you go on what matters most to you, and the more zoomed-out a perspective you can bring to the task at hand or the overall goal you're seeking, the more readily you'll be able to determine "how important is that, really?" If it really is important, it's certainly worth pursuing the solution with a seeker's mindset, not one fearfully focused on past mistakes. If it's "just a little thing" then maybe you can examine your priorities and shuffle them around a bit, not as a matter of resignation but as a matter of simply acknowledging that sometimes we want something "just because," even though it's not really that big a deal. Just because we have a preference doesn't mean that not yet having met it has to ruin our day.

Once again, being patient with yourself and others is of utmost importance. The brain's job is to compare not only where you are to where you'd like to be, but to also compare, for example, how soon you "should have gotten there" to how long it's taken you so far. The brain will compare you not only to others around you but to people you don't even know. It may be projecting a standard of what or where you'd prefer to be, compared to some unmet preferences and desires your brain may generate after watching a TV advertisement. Because your brain knows every detail of your own history on the same or similar matters, it may generate thoughts of self-torment (at not "getting there" yet, even during times you succeeded, or perhaps not as well as you'd have preferred).

Note that these thoughts may have no basis in reality whatsoever; little more than that long-standing voice in your head that echoes from a comment made long ago by a fellow third grader you thought was your friend, or perhaps a parent, former boss, or an old romantic partner.

What's required to get from where you are to where you'd prefer to be, first and foremost, is to put yourself in the best mindset to work on resolving the issue. Notice the comparison taking place and give yourself and your brain a hug if it needs that. The brain must compare where it thinks you are relative to whatever it can create in the moment. Nothing personal! Your real job, as The Real You, is to remember that if your brain creates some catastrophic scenario, it can be quite convincing, but it's just pumping out thought, which is its job! You wouldn't ask your heart to stop pumping blood, your lungs to stop pumping air, or your stomach to stop pumping stomach acid, right? It's just your brain pumping out thought, and thank goodness, you're not your brain, you're the noticer of it! When you're standing in The Real You place you'll be much more able to stay on the challenging path toward resolving even the toughest issue.

CHAPTER SEVEN

REFINE

If you've legitimately done all you can to resolve an issue, and it just won't resolve, it's time to *refine* who you're being about the thing you can't resolve. I have a couple of exes. I get along great with the first one, but the second one not so much. I have, however, so completely refined who I'm being when we communicate now that what used to wipe me out is now teaching material for this book!

Mark Twain said "Comparison is the death of joy."

To this I'll add: "Awareness is the death of comparison."

The key element in this refinement is to remember that refinement, too, is a process and potentially a long-term process at that. How long? What part of you wants to know that bit of comparative detail (which is, of course, the source of displeasure about any bumps and curves on the road to refinement!)? Whether we're refining metal into higher levels of purity, or our character into higher levels of awareness, courage, and resiliency, it takes time, patience, care, and effort. As soon as you step into the place of noticing—into the place of awareness that there's an issue about which you have a Point A and a Point B—do a quick self-study on why your Point B is a Point B for you! Why is that unmet preference or need important to you? Why is that unfulfilled expectation important to you? What's missing that you wish was there? What's there that you wish was missing? What's the end result you're seeking? What does that look like? What does it feel like? What's required on your part to get there? One of the biggest pieces we must find (more like discovering than finding something that was lost, because it's already in there, remember?), hold on to, and keep with us always when times are toughest, especially when we're in the thick of that stuff to which we're applying the refinement process, is courage.

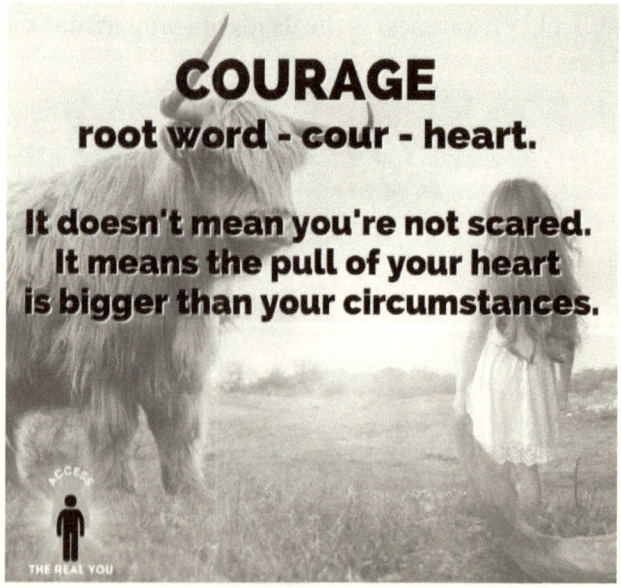

Courage isn't being unafraid of something that's legitimately frightening. Courage is not blindly and mindlessly charging into a potentially dangerous situation. It's about accessing your heart and tuning into its wisdom, insight, and that which pulls you forward—not merely avoiding something that pushes you into circumstances that perhaps are not even meant for you.

Allow me to get real-world and deeply personal about refinement. I'll give you my favorite example: my second son's mom. She was for many years the Exemplar of Exasperation, the Beast of Button Pushing, and the bane of my existence, until I realized that her manipulation of me was my work, not hers, and that I was allowing her to push me around with her words and actions. I was the one allowing my brain chatter—filled with a superfluous abundance of historical evidence amplified by a wealth of worry about a soon-forthcoming future incident I was already trying to avoid or felt like I was already trapped within—to completely take me over.

And that whole button-pushing story I'd been telling myself and everyone who'd listen, was also all on me! After stepping back, zooming out, working on resolving *my* issues after our issues remained unresolved, I came to understand with all my heart and soul that all of my buttons were based on *my* wounds and *my* woundedness. I experienced the truth that every inch of the wiring of those buttons attached to my bioenergetic systems was a direct result of the extent to which I had not yet processed and worked through all of my own wounds and woundedness. The resulting neurological circuitry and all of its perfectly imperfect design was all mine and completely messed up. I realized, when I finally learned the Point A—Point B distinction and began applying The Real You principles and the self-knowledge I learned from that self-study, that my ex-wife was just "over there being who she is," and I was the one pushing all of my own &^%*&$ buttons! AAAARRRRGGGHHHH (with celebration at this epiphany!)!

Example of refinement around my ex-wife: This process took several years (in case your brain was wondering how long it took) for me to finally master. I hadn't fully realized and refined The Real You principles yet. If I had, it might still have taken a while, but the years of suffering I put myself through might have been reduced to days or weeks or perhaps months, but certainly not years.

Because my ex worked a nine-to-five job, and I was self-employed (another way of saying I worked at all times of the day and night to make room in my schedule for my son), I picked up our son from school two to five days each week for almost a decade. Every day, just before or just after I'd pick him up, I'd get a phone call from her. In his elementary school days that call was just before 3:00 p.m., as I was sitting in the long car line. My caller ID would show me it was her and, as much as I didn't want to answer the call, I did. Her ring tone, for the record, was the same sound as the "red alert" in the old Star Trek series (not exactly a way to calm down and prepare myself for the onslaught of verbiage I knew I was about to receive).

I'd immediately hear, "Are you there yet?!"

Her voice was rarely, if ever, calm and usually substantially more than a bit urgent. Looking back on the whole phenomenon from my current perspective (grounded in The Real You principles), I'm sure that because my brain's circuitry was already shifting into a hyper-overdrive mix of worry, anger, frustration, and an overarching cloud of doom and gloom by 2:55 p.m., every afternoon. Just seeing it was her calling was enough to melt me down before I'd even answered the phone! She was likely just asking, because she couldn't help herself, and really did want to make sure I was there on time to get our son, but I took it as an insult to my intelligence, my character, and my fatherhood. Every. Single. Time.

I'd say, "It's three o'clock, and I haven't called to let you and/or the school know that neither I nor my car has died or something, so yes, of course I'm here!" Things would quickly escalate into her ordering me to make sure every one of several items were handled to her satisfaction— required books, papers, etc., in his backpack; making sure he ate all of his lunch (which always got the obligatory grade-schooler answer, "Of course, dad," with the requisite eye roll and as condescending a tone as a third grader could muster, which, of course, I'd brain-generated that he'd learned from his mother); making sure he had all of his clothes that he was wearing when he got to school, and anything else she could come up with in that always-more-tense-than-I'd-prefer moment. I was always and immediately on edge for a variety of reasons:

- We were divorced because she drove me, quite literally, to a breaking point—from which I'd not yet completely recovered, and about which I was still in therapy—either about her, about my damaged relationship with our son, or about the romantic relationship I was in at the time, which I was never going to discuss with her.

- Our son was classic ADD—incredibly brilliant, but forgetful and eminently distractible—so it was pretty much expected that some papers, clothing, or other items would be forgotten every day, and I was not about to get out of the car line with my son, find a place to park a few hundred yards away, go back into the school with him, which would be totally embarrassing to him, meet each of his teachers to determine what he had and didn't have, and then get back into the far end of the car line over a piece of clothing or paper that he could collect the next day. If it wasn't an urgent matter, like exam preparation or pieces of a science project in process, I simply refused to make an elementary school matter an urgent one, no matter what it was. Because he was diagnosed and classified a "Section 504" kid (the legal statute allowing for him to receive specific school accommodations for his ADD diagnosis), there was precious little that would classify as real emergency, thus anything my ex would say was already filtered through my brain-generated microfilter that would, at that point, have prevented even a series of heartfelt compliments from her to have made it through into my conscious awareness.

Anyway, you can probably guess by now that the conversation would soon descend into some sort of "you must!" orders from her, followed by the obligatory, "you need to calm down!" from me, and her equally reactive, "Calm down?! This is our son's schoolwork we're talking about! You want him to fail?! This is his life!"

Then I'd drop the calm but assertive, "If you don't calm down, I'm going to hang up." She would, of course, start to go bonkers, and "click," I'd hang up.

Then I'd look up into the sky and yell at the top of my lungs (sometimes actually hurting my vocal chords), "C'MON GOD, WHY THE HELL DOES THIS HAVE TO KEEP HAPPENING TO ME?! I'M A GOOD GUY AND GOOD DAD AND DID MY BEST TO BE A GOOD HUSBAND! WHAT THE HELL?!"

Fast forward almost eight years—after I'd learned The Real You principles, how to be the noticer, and how to drop those Point As and Point Bs into that Bowl of Awareness, and work on resolve-refine-release (don't worry, we'll get to "release" soon enough). My son is about to get out of his international baccalaureate high school classes. It's 4 p.m., and school is out at 4:15 p.m., and I'm not in a car line this time, which is very much longer than the elementary school car line because there are 3500 students at his presidential blue ribbon international baccalaureate school. I'm parked across the street so he can effortlessly walk to my car, and we can stay away from the crowd altogether, but I still get the phone call, right on time, at 4:10 p.m.

"Are you there yet? Make sure he has all of his homework and supplies for all of his projects! He's dozens of homework assignments behind and hasn't even started any of the TEN projects he's behind on! YOU MAKE SURE TO NOT JUST ASK HIM BUT TO MAKE HIM SHOW YOU THAT HE HAS EVERYTHING, AND IF HE DOESN'T, MAKE SURE HE GOES BACK AND GETS EVERYTHING HE NEEDS!"

And once again, I'd say, albeit now in a much calmer voice than the one I used all those years of progress ago, "It's all going to be fine. We'll work on what he has, I'll fix him dinner, get him home at a reasonable hour, and it'll all be fine."

"Fine? FINE?! ARE YOU LISTENING TO ME AT ALL?! HE'S SO FAR BEHIND HE MIGHT NOT GRADUATE THIS YEAR! HE'S NOT SLEEPING WELL, AND HE'S LIVING IN STRESS!"

"You really need to calm down. Given your level of intensity, that might be contributing to his stress and lack of good sleep. I'll talk to him as soon as he gets into the car, and I'll make sure he has everything he needs."

"WHAT?! LIKE WE CAN TRUST HIM TO TELL US THE TRUTH?!"

"He always tells me the truth when I ask him a direct question and let him give me a direct answer."

"YOU NEED TO MAKE SURE HE HAS EVERYTHING AND THAT HE'S REALLY GETTING IT DONE!"

"You need to calm down or I'm going to hang up. I am not required to let you yell at me any longer, remember? I've set that boundary, and I really will not let you cross that line with me any longer."

"BUT YOU NEED TO . . ."

"Click," and I hang up. . . . for the 1,857th time.

Except now, armed with the tools available to me in The Real You principles, I now look symbolically up at God above (again, no religion here . . . I know my divinity lives within me always in all ways), smile a big smile, and say, "Wow! That's about the two hundreth day in a row I didn't let her get to me! How am I doing, God?!"

And I could feel God touch my heart with, "You're doing great, beautiful soul! You're practicing The Real You principles I've shown you. You're setting boundaries and insisting they be honored or you'll disengage. You're remaining more calm than ever. You're not letting her push your buttons any more. You've made wonderful progress!"

Progress! Progress is a process, and this was not an instantaneous process. I loved myself enough to give myself a break when I felt like I'd failed on whatever myriad of scenarios my brain would create—even after I'd learned The Real You principles, because I realized that it still takes time to diligently practice and habituate The Real You principles. Even then, you may perhaps master those principles for some people you see regularly, and others may still hook you in the most frustrating way. And that's OK! As soon as you can catch yourself having "messed it up again," breathe in to five and out to eight, four times, apologize if need be to whomever may have borne the brunt of your reactionary forgetfulness, and move on! Breathe some more if necessary. Smile a big smile for a while. Then "get back on the horse," as the old expression goes.

Let's face it, the more important the issue and the more crushingly crucial your much-sought result is to you, the harder it hits you, and the more work is required. And (good news—bad news alert) the more refined you've become about the issues you've been unable to resolve, the more clearly you can see what remains for you to refine in those other areas!

Here's the next Real You principle: *please remember that if you can see an area in your life that still needs work, this is a clear demonstration that you've come far enough in your progress to see that! Love yourself. Forgive yourself. Keep walking.* It does get better, even if it's in Divine timing and not your desired timing. Remember that, relative to divinity, time and space are nonexistent . . . so what feels like ages for us is but a blink in eternity. Remember the old, "This too shall pass" verse? I hate to admit it, but there's something to that one. We may never actually resolve some issues, but we can refine who we're being about the things we can't resolve. And after we've legitimately done all we can to refine who we're being about the things we can't resolve, there's still one last, very important step we can take: We can Release what remains.

CHAPTER EIGHT

RELEASE

You've done all you can to resolve an issue, and it just won't resolve; you've done all you can do and be to refine who you are about the issue that won't resolve, and there are still nagging pieces floating around in your awareness. Time to *release* what remains. How do you do this? We'll cover this in a moment, but here's an example from my life that I use when discussing release.

In January and February 2018, I lost both of my parents. Mom had gotten very ill with some sort of flu and Dad, having micromanaged Mom's care for years, had finally reached the end of his rope both physically and emotionally. They were, after all, 84 and 88, respectively, and dad could only do so much, which was already a ton given my mother's steadily declining health. Dad called the ambulance which, in their small town in south Louisiana, didn't take long to arrive. The paramedics got Mom on the gurney and into the ambulance. When they looked at Dad, they pointed out that he didn't look well either and insisted he hop in with them and come along to the hospital.

After they got Mom settled into her room on one end of the hospital, the doctors examined Dad and told him he had pneumonia and needed to be checked in immediately as well. So, they had Mom in one end of the hospital and Dad on the other. My father, never one to remain calm about much of anything, worked himself into such a fit over his being prevented from micromanaging Mom's care as he always had that he had a massive stroke and died that first night in the hospital.

When the medical staff finally got Mom stabilized a few days later, and she had her wits about her again, she asked where her husband was, and they gave her the horrible news. She was so devastated that she literally willed herself to death over the next several weeks, transitioning out a month after Dad had gone; the dates bookending their sixty-third wedding anniversary.

I loved my parents. We had our not-so-pretty moments, but the last decade or so of our time together was beautiful. We'd all done a lot of work on ourselves, had resolved most of the issues we'd had to deal with, refined away most of the other rough spots, and were comfortable letting the rest go. Their passing so close together was shocking and emotionally devastating. I couldn't resolve their deaths; they were gone—at once and without any warning—and there was nothing I could do about it. I couldn't seem to refine enough of what remained, because I love my parents and I always will. Our relationship was challenging at times, but we always knew that we loved each other and, considering how great the last bunch of years were with them, this was just brutal. Remember, "it always hurts exactly as much as you care?" I'd visited a couple of times a year and had called two or three times every week since my college years. Losing both of them in such short order, and with Dad's passing such a huge shock since he was by far the healthier and more clear-headed of the two, was just horrible. Those two or three times a week I'd normally be calling to check in were the times when I now reached for the phone and realized I had to put it down. Those times after big football games when I'd call Dad just to hear him rant for half an hour about the lousy calls by the referees, or hear about the latest great shot hit by a tennis player, or a magical putt by a golfer he'd just watched, were gone in an instant, never to return.

And those times I'd call Mom and fill her in on the latest news about my sons—her only grandsons—she would want to celebrate all of the smallest details with me on every single call. We both looked forward to those calls, and now all I had left were her usual phrases, uttered with the thickest, slowest southern drawl you've ever heard: "Faaabulous," or "That's Wooonduhful, Huuuun," when something good had happened, and "Hawwwrruhs!" when something bad had happened.

I missed them terribly for days, then weeks, then months. What remained, even years later, was to simply release those feelings of emptiness. But how?

Here's an example. Again, I know you're reading a book but please engage with this very important experiential example.

Find something nearby that you can drop from a height of several feet that won't break or roll away.

Found it? Good! Now play along, OK? If you actually do this, it'll make a profound impact, I promise!

Stand up or sit tall in your chair, hold that object in your hand, hold your arm out fully extended, palm down, and open your hand and let the object fall.

That is release. In case you didn't quite get it yet, play along.

Pick it back up, hold the object in your hand again, hold your arm out fully extended, palm down, and open your hand and let the object fall again.

That is release.

Let's cover what just happened in detail. When you opened your hand, you opened up all of your fingers at once and the object fell to the ground. Notice that you didn't allow any of your fingers to stay closed, holding on to the object. You didn't think about what was required to do so, or why or how or when or where. You simply opened up your hand, releasing with all fingers the object you were holding, allowing it to fall.

Consider your fingers to be the brain-generated conditions that we often require to be resolved before we can fully release, and consider the object you were holding to be some person or concern or circumstance that you've been unable, or perhaps unwilling, to let go of for whatever your reasons may be. We know by now that the brain is a vital organ whose job it is, for the purpose of The Real You conversation, to pump out thoughts just as the stomach pumps out stomach acid. We know that the brain must separate all thoughts about everything from everything else, and that there will always be some comparison-based Point A vs. Point B which may be noticed, and that there will thus always be something being generated by the brain which must be either resolved, refined, or released. Given this knowledge, would you ever expect yourself to be free of conditions to be met that would ever allow you to have nothing remaining to release? This is why when it's time to release something, you must symbolically open your hand and let it (whatever "it" is) go. There's no other way.

Simple but not easy, right? Especially when it's something as huge as a dear relationship or other life aspect that means so much to you! Here's a prime example for you to chew on: *forgiveness is release.* Before we can truly forgive someone (or ourselves, for goodness' sake!), we must release any and all conditions, thoughts, and anything about the person that must be forgiven. Another "simple but not easy" one, right?

There's a story about Jesus (I promise, we're not getting into religion here, but I love this example) where he's talking with his disciples about forgiveness, and one of the guys (I'm no biblical scholar, so I can't tell you which one) says, "Look, Jesus, I've been working really hard on this forgiveness thing, and I think I'm really doing great. But then I see this guy around town who really gets my goat [possibly literally, given the time period!]. I think I've forgiven him, then he pulls one of his stunts, and I'm back to being angry with him again! HOW MANY TIMES AM I GOING TO HAVE TO FORGIVE THIS GUY BEFORE THIS FORGIVENESS THING REALLY STICKS?! IT'S WEARING ME OUT, JESUS!!!"

Jesus, in his inimitable fashion, answers with a very symbolic answer: "My brother, you're going to have to forgive him seventy times seven times." Seventy times seven?! This did not mean that the disciple was to forgive the man 490 times, but then had permission to beat him up and down once and for all. Seventy times seven was a symbolic way of Jesus telling his student and friend, "Brother, you're just going to have to keep forgiving him for as long as it takes, even if it takes the rest of your life."

"WHAT?" you may be asking. "I'm supposed to JUST KEEP ON FORGIVING the ones who wear me out and DRIVE ME FREAKING CRAZY?"

Yep.

Here's an even bigger one for most people: Whom do you know more about than anyone on earth? Yourself. Are you willing to go back over your entire life and forgive yourself for everything you've ever done? For every mistake you've ever made? For everything you've ever spoken in anger or sadness or frustration or disappointment? If not, what remains is staining your insides and likely contributing to some physical/psychological/emotional dis-ease.

Again, no religion here, just a powerful lesson and some perspective. The Old Testament, which Jesus learned, studied, and regularly presented for discussion and teaching as the rabbi that he was, contained 613 "commandments" that, in my opinion, were not necessarily meant to be "rules" or "laws" to be followed, as much as 613 ways to bring God/Creator/Divine Consciousness into our daily lives. At one point in the New Testament (again, I'm no scholar, but I remember the gist of the story and its applicable lesson), some smarty-pants guy confronted Jesus, determined to trip him up and embarrass him in front of a lot of people. The guy asked, "OK, Rabbi, what's the most important commandment in the Bible?" Jesus remembered instantly one of the two prayers spoken in every Jewish worship service—one is where it's written, "Hear O Israel, the Lord our God is One," and the other prayer opens with, "You will love the Lord Your God with all your heart, with all your soul, and with all your might." Jesus applied these in his answer. He told the man that the single most important commandment in the Old Testament was, "Love the Lord your God with all your heart, soul, strength, and mind, and the second part, which is the same as the first, is to *love your neighbor as you love yourself.*"

Let's face it. When we're at our very best, most of us can much more easily forgive others than forgive ourselves, right? Especially with all the guilt-tripping implemented by brain-ruled Judeo-Christian teachers and control-based clergy over the centuries. The whole thing about our inherent imperfection requiring either a redeemer, who has yet to arrive to save us all (Judaism), is released by the point that Jesus made clear: the best we can do is to work on ourselves first, or we'll be projecting our mess onto others all along our life-path.

Forgiveness of ourselves is an inside job, and forgiving others is no more or less an inside job. My second ex-wife drove me crazy until I learned to forgive her for being who she was being. It was, after all, where she was at that time, had been for a while, and might just always be where'd she be! It was apparent to me what "her work" needed to be, but would she ever see it? And if she did see it, was she ready, willing, and able to do her work? That was not for me to judge, to do for her, or to ask her to do. It was her work, not mine. Likewise, if she bothered me or attacked me, that was on her too. My work was to resolve the issues I had with her, to refine who I'd been being about it if we couldn't resolve it, and to release what remained as many times as necessary to achieve *personal* peace of mind. Seventy times seven indeed!

So how do we ever accomplish this? Love. *Unconditional* love. Unconditional love is, by definition, the release of conditions that may otherwise prevent you from loving yourself and loving others. Of course, there will always be a history that your brain has stored covering every detail used to justify your anger, sadness, disappointment, and pain. Of course, there will always be reasons used to justify how you feel, which can keep you stuck in the poisonous and self-destructive soup that characterizes a lack of self-forgiveness and forgiveness of others, and a lack of self-love and love of others. What you carry in this area will, I assure you, lead to discomfort and eventually to dis-ease if you do not release it and walk the way of love and self-love, forgiveness and self-forgiveness, for as many moments in every day as you can remember them.

Love is the only way out.

And what of *YOU*? Who in your life has upset you? Who has brought you pain, anger, sadness, disappointment, and frustration? Have you done your work? Use the tools you've been given here. Implement the Point A vs. Point B process, then notice and study for yourself what makes that Point B a Point B for you. Do your work around resolving, refining, and releasing, and please remember that your work never ends. Ever. As long as you have a brain generating thoughts about everything, you'll have work to do. You can have it be something "you've got to do," or you can have it be something rewarding that "you get to do." You can have it be time taken for yourself so you can be all you're here to be and have your life be as wonderful as it can be for you and for everyone around you. You can also, as Alan Watts suggested, make it play instead of work, which, as challenging as it may be, will be more fun and more rewarding if you have it be play. Are there past communications that you've spoken or were spoken to you about which you still carry a "coulda, woulda, shoulda"? I know it's no fun to look at these things, but now you have some useful tools to finally get you past them all. *Every Single One.*

Resolve—refine—release. These are the ways to be about any issue that naturally and effortlessly arise in the Awareness that you are.

We all want to resolve issues, but when we can't resolve them, even after determined effort in the ways mentioned earlier, are we willing to do the inner work required to refine who we've been being about the things we can't resolve? If, after diligently working with our unresolvable and even unrefinable issues, we still have work to do, are we willing to do the ongoing and sometimes challenging work of releasing what remains? The work we do for ourselves impacts the quality of every relationship in which we will ever find ourselves. When Jesus said, "Love your neighbor as you love yourself," he understood that any unhealed wounds we carry will affect us in ways we may not understand or of which we are aware. Muhammad is said to have spoken, "If a man be at peace with you, you must reach out your hand in peace to him." What if the guy is the one who hurt you yesterday and now seeks friendship and forgiveness? Hard, right? If we do not love ourselves enough to do the inner work required to heal ourselves, our wounds may come out as reactivity instead of responsiveness. Those "button pushing" episodes, to which we are all susceptible, are dramatically reduced in both intensity and frequency when we take the time to resolve, refine, and release. In the Awareness that we are, tuning in to that deeper, often hidden or compartmentalized part of ourselves, we can bear loving witness to our own imperfections, frailties, and shortcomings and love ourselves not just with them and in spite of them, but *through* and *past* them. Forgiveness of yourself and others is so important, I'll add it as one of The Real You principles:

Forgiveness releases you from the bondage of your unfulfilled expectations. All of the pieces of this resolve-refine-release process are simple but not easy. "Love your neighbor as you love yourself" is simple but not easy. Love and self-love, forgiveness and self-forgiveness are simple but not easy. Remembering this truth may not make any of the steps easier, but my intention is that you remember, when you are troubled, that it is not The Real You that is troubled. Rather, it is your brain that is generating troublesome thoughts that may be Noticed, studied within The Real You principles, studied within the Point A—Point B framework as a matter of self-exploration and self-excavation, and be resolved, or provide work for your refinement, or be released as often as required for your inner peace to become your Way. (I hear your brain doubting and being cynical or sarcastic—it's OK. I forgive you!)

CHAPTER NINE

CONTEXT, AND A PART OF YOUR LIKELY FORGOTTEN HISTORY

If we were to take hundreds of laser pointers in a completely darkened room, and we directed all of them to touch all of the points comprising a common object, like a coffee mug, we would see, as all of the points of light began to touch the various parts of the mug, the shape of the object. The catch here, however, is that the points of light can only tell us the shape of the object. Without proper context, and knowing from our own experience what a coffee mug looks like and how to make best use of it, we cannot know what we're actually seeing regardless of how effectively it is shown us. (Even then, before we've had our morning coffee, we still might not be certain!).

The brain will, under any circumstance, generate (often, completely erroneously) context as well as content, and the content will usually be derived from and influenced by the context. "Where we're coming from" alters our perceptions of things we experience and even the people with whom we're interacting. Ever go to a sporting event with someone who didn't know anything about the sport and was just there to hang out with the crowd? How about going to a museum with a friend to see your favorite artist's work, and the person only went to be with you and doesn't even begin to understand what you're so excited about? Likewise, a fan of one sports team can watch the same play as a fan of the opposing sports team and see a completely different result, especially in case of a rule being broken or where the outcome of the game might be impacted. Context is crucial. Here's another Real You principle to chew on: *Context is the background from which reality and perception—and those two are more related than most realize—occur.*

Now, let me give you a real-life example of how the brain works with every-day stimuli (content) and how perspective and your own personal history (context) affect your perception. Let's go back to that billboard analogy. Billboards and all media influence in powerful ways, but I'm specifically using billboards because they are visual only.

When we notice a billboard, there's the obvious aspect of what's presented to us (content) that immediately goes through a sort of automatic internal analysis. Yet there's also a wealth of other connective/creative/responsive internal content being generated by our brains that, in turn, is being generated to fit within an also-brain-generated context that is itself a product of the entirety of our past experiences, present experiences, and perhaps even an anticipated future. Our brains are doing this *all day, every day*, whether we're awake or asleep, conscious or unconscious. The brain is the depository for all that we see, hear, smell, taste, and touch, as well as the source of how we think about and process all that content. How we end up feeling and believing about it all is directly affected by our brain-created *context*. Twenty people can see the same thing and even go out and buy the same product they saw on the billboard. But each, if you asked them what they thought about the billboard and what happened in their minds when they saw it, would likely give you a different sequence of related thoughts. Remember, too, that the brain is a vital organ that never stops. From your birth until now, it has never stopped and never will until you're gone. Never underestimate how it affects perception.

Now, let's back up a bit—all the way back.

Before you were born, you were peaceful, happy, calm, and quiet inside your mom's belly until, quite suddenly, you were squeezed and contorted, pushed, and popped out into the world, awakening to an entirely different set of circumstances than those to which you'd grown accustomed for those many months. Perhaps you got intensely squeezed in a way not at all pleasant, nor in any way comfortable or familiar. You popped out of your mom, or perhaps popped out by a C-section. The doctor slapped your bottom. You took your first deep breath, and there you were—bright lights in your eyes, still feeling the sting and shock of just having been slapped on your bottom, still recovering from the huge discomfort at being removed from your comfy floating peace. And now there were all these new stimuli happening all at once! People all around you laughing and crying and hugging and yelling and cheering, and your brain, which perceives and attempts to understand all of these stimuli, went into overwhelm at that moment, and has been, to some degree, in hyper-observation-and-process-it-all-at-once mode ever since.

Want some context? Most of us have been walking, talking reactions, on some level about some things, for our entire lives. Most of what we're freaking out about started on our birthdays. I can't tell you how many people I've met who've told me that under hypnosis they were brought to an awareness of some sort of birth-related trauma. From Day One, some of us really are deeply affected and are still swimming in, so to speak, the context grounded in the occurrences on our actual birthdays.

Then we could talk about birthdays and birthday parties. Some may be remembered as wonderful, but some not so much. Are you feeling stressed just reading this and remembering what happened to you on that not-so-great birthday? Breathe. Smile a big smile. It's OK. It feels wonderful, or it feels terrible, for the same reason: because you care so much that it turns out the way you want! Want to know why it's OK even if it feels horrible? Because you are not your brain or the body that has a brain in it that's pumping out thoughts about it all, you are the noticer of these!

Then we could talk about all of those possibly unpleasant, possibly legitimately traumatizing events of our respective childhoods. The bad news is that so many people we meet every day—perhaps ourselves included—are walking around with the traumas we experienced early in life. Those events are still living bioenergetically in the very cells in our bodies, and they are still affecting present-day perceptions and behaviors. Once again, however, there's some good news: You are not your brain. You are the noticer of it, and in the noticer place, all may become teaching material to be resolved, refined, or released.

CHAPTER TEN

MORE TOOLS TO FACILITATE GROWING THE AWARENESS THAT YOU ARE

Even when we think we are present to all that is happening in our brains, bodies, and circumstances, the brain's ability to process input and to accurately perceive is, in fact, quite variable, and not at all consistent. We may think we're seeing something quite clearly when, in fact, we are not. What we have going on in our minds may sometimes act as a filter, modifier, suppressor, or even as a denier of truth. Another example of how powerful and often unconscious context can be gets applied right here, right now.

One thing to drop into your Awareness toolbox is the Principle of Closure.

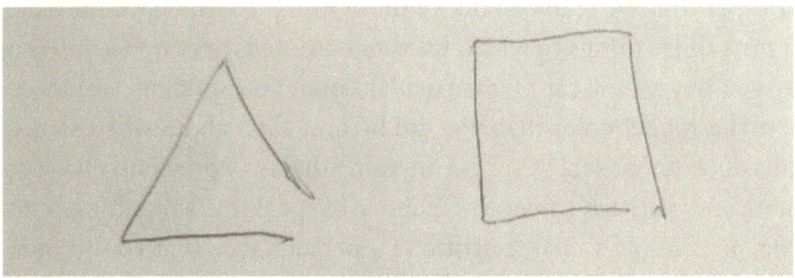

Notice the shapes above. Most will certainly see these as a triangle and a square, though they are not quite completely formed as such. Our brains will, because we already know (background context) what a triangle and square look like (content), fill in the small gaps and complete the shape as we would expect, based on our experiences. If there's something missing, our brains provide what's missing. If, however, there's something ADDED, our brains have a much harder time.

Notice the shapes below.

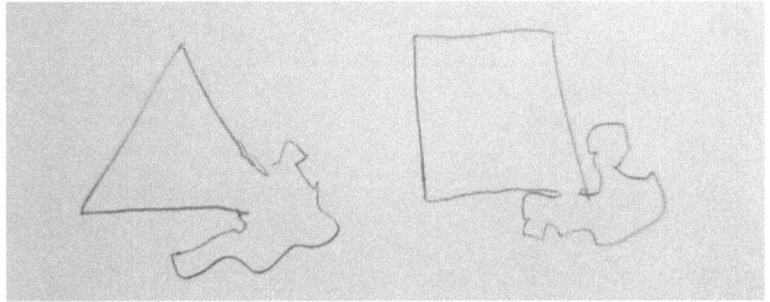

Notice the difference? When presented with an "almost triangle" or an "almost square," there's almost no way not to see the triangle and the square as "just a triangle" and "just a square." Our brains can fill in what's missing as naturally as breathing. Trying to pretend some added squiggles aren't there, attached to the shapes with which we are already familiar, is nearly impossible! Notice that!

Apply this to almost any circumstance in our lives, and you may find it challenging to see beyond the obvious to what may actually be right in front of you. We really do notice those things to which we are attuned and miss those things to which we're not attuned. Ever notice how right after you buy a new car of a particular color, you suddenly see more of that make/model/color than you did before? How about when someone points out some aspect of almost anything that may previously have gone unnoticed—perhaps someone's manner of speaking, something in their stride, or possibly a characteristic of a person's face that you'd not seen before. Is there any way not to notice it once pointed out? No way, right?! The degree to which we may miss things that are right in front of us is sometimes surprising. Take the following images as a prime example. You may see "it" immediately, but most do not.

You are the the BEST XX	We are the the BEST XX

Read out loud what you see in the left box. (I know it's a book! Play along!)

Read out loud what you see in the right box. (Come on! Play along!)

Read both of these out loud again.

Obvious, right? What's in each box is obvious. The words are, after all, printed on the page.

Now, get a pen or pencil and read each word in each box, touching each word with the pen or pencil as you read them aloud.

Pretty wild, isn't it? I first saw this done in a room of 200 people—only a handful saw it from the outset. Bottom line: We see what we expect to see, and we experience what we expect to experience! See how easy it is to miss something, even when it's something this obvious? Imagine how easy it is to miss something less obvious! Imagine how many other pieces of your daily life you might be missing!

How "real" does reality feel now?!

Here's another example of the fact that your brain will generate stimuli even in the absence of stimuli! My high school science teacher once took a pen-style laser pointer (quite the cool toy in the late 1970s), pointed it at the wall, and then turned the classroom's light off. After about ten seconds, the light settled down when he quit moving it around. About thirty to forty-five seconds after that, I noticed the light had started wiggling around a bit. He asked us to describe what the light-dot was doing, and we all described a similar bouncing and moving phenomenon. It was as if he was very minutely and very rapidly jostling his laser pointer around, or perhaps that his hands were simply a bit jittery. Shortly thereafter, he turned the classroom lights back on and, much to our surprise, he had laid the laser pointer on his desk, and the pointer hadn't even moved since he'd put it down on his desk only seconds after he'd turned the lights out! What had happened to everyone in the class—all twenty-five of us— was that our brains had literally created motion, manipulating our eye muscles, when no external movement had even happened!

Now apply this lesson to any time your brain isn't currently occupied. How much are you noticing when there's nothing actually happening? How many thoughts about others, yourself, or circumstances might your brain be generating at this very moment that have nothing to do with anything and are just "space filler" generated by your brain to keep you and it occupied?!

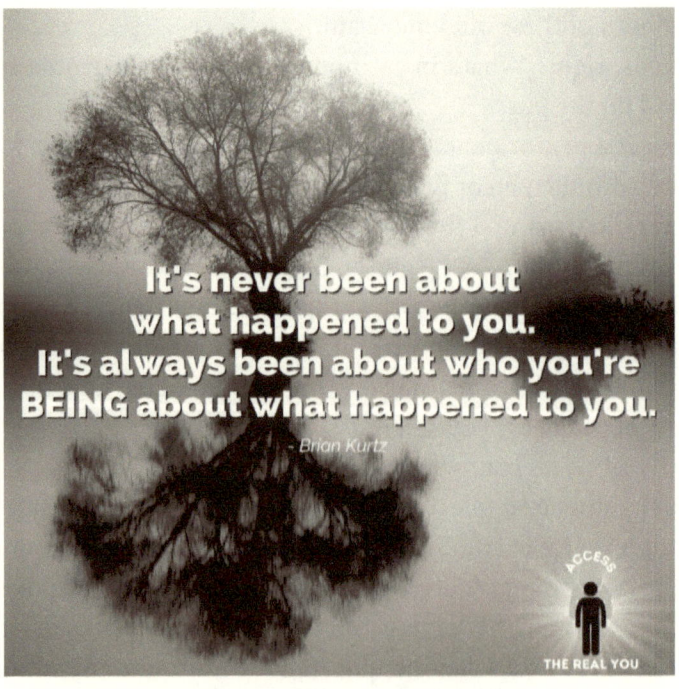

It's never been about
what happened to you.
It's always been about who you're
BEING about what happened to you.

- Brian Kurtz

Now, if you're willing, begin to review any place in your life that you've found yourself certain about something, only to find that things weren't as expected. Because our brains (not The Real You) require certainty and full-on justification of our points of view, when things don't turn out as we expect or prefer. We may be left feeling confused, distressed, or some other "less-than-comfy" feeling. Notice that! Remember, too, in these moments, that any of these are just thoughts generated by your brain and are not you.

Why did that person do what he did? Why did she say what she said? Why did those people act toward you the way they did? Can you ask these questions with genuine curiosity, and desire for self-exploration without requiring an easy, immediate answer? Even more challenging, can you accept that what you infer from information gathered might be incomplete or even altogether incorrect? As the above images often prove out, even the most obvious things we see, hear, touch, taste, smell, and feel could actually be completely incorrect!

The point of this is not to cause you concern. The concerns are brain generated and are not The Real You anyway! The point is to make you aware that things are not always what they seem. To generalize this out to the rest of your life is nothing more than a gentle reminder to love yourself and to love others. Things we may consider obvious may not be so obvious to others. The things that others may consider obvious may make no sense to us at all! How we feel about some people, circumstances, cultural phenomena, habits, etc. may not at all be how others feel about these same things. Are you a sports fan? I grew up in south Louisiana as a diehard New Orleans Saints fan, and we had culturally ingrained into us by our sports information media a vehement dislike for not only the Atlanta Falcons football team, but for their fans as well. Imagine how I felt finding out that a dear friend in college, who happened to be from Atlanta, was a diehard Falcons fan?! Once we got to know each other as fellow humans beyond our preferred sports teams, we became close friends. But how many other parts of your life are inherently divisive? How many of our relationships are affected by our culturally ingrained biases? Matters like nationality, race, religion, sexual preference, political party, and a host of others can distort our viewpoints about fellow human souls.

Please remember that the brain's job is to separate, categorize, analyze, and otherwise divide everything, everyone, and all of our experiences and thoughts about all of these into bits to be stored by the brain for later. We may indeed have many distorted viewpoints occurring far more often than we'd be willing to admit, polluted with misperceptions, judgments, biases, and outright prejudice toward people, places, circumstances, and most other aspects of our lives. The best we can do is to be aware that this phenomenon exists and might possibly be affecting every aspect of our lives. Remember that everyone has their own set of life experiences, and that each and every one of those experiences has left indelible marks in their brains, all of which are filtered through their own histories. The collection of their experienced perceptions affect how they see you and everything else in their lives, including themselves!

Confused? Concerned? Worried? Angry? Frustrated? Disappointed? Notice that! All of these are just thoughts generated by your brain that mean nothing in particular. Apply the Point A and Point B to all issues, past, present, and future, as well as establishing where along the resolve-refine-release process they are, and breathe and smile as often as serves you.

How else can we be about that? We can be loving and self-loving, forgiving and self-forgiving, being the noticer of all we think and feel and experience. We can stand in that noticer place where, in the inherent stillness of that Presence, our Divine Nature is more readily able to receive and share through us, as us, that which is ours to receive and share in any given moment.

Until you make the unconscious conscious, it will direct your life, and you will call it fate.

--*Carl Jung*

How many of your life's circumstances are you still carrying within you? How many wounds are still deeply ingrained in the very cells that make up your body?

Here's an applicable quote from author, lawyer, and all-around amazing woman Iyanla Vanzant: "Until you heal the wounds of your past, you are going to bleed. You can bandage the bleeding with food, with alcohol, with drugs, with work, with cigarettes, with sex; but eventually, it will all ooze through and stain your life. You must find the strength to open the wounds, stick your hands inside, pull out the core of the pain that is holding you in your past—the memories—and make peace with them."

Deeply ingrained within us also flow thoughts, often imperceptible in our moment-by-moment awareness, that I call the "thought undercurrent."

CHAPTER ELEVEN

THE THOUGHT UNDERCURRENT

One of the things you'll notice as you become a more frequent noticer of your brain chatter is what I call the "thought undercurrent." This is the never-ending flow of thoughts that over the course of a day (or week, or year, or lifetime) can greatly enhance your life or greatly slow you down. Remember that if you don't release or consciously process the thoughts your brain is generating, there will soon be corresponding chemicals generated by the brain and in the body. If your thought undercurrent is generally happy, loving, optimistic, and kind, your body will over time reflect this thought undercurrent. If, however, your thought undercurrent is generally concerned, anxious, and bearing the weight of the world's upheaval amid the massive changes taking place socially, politically, economically, etc., your body will begin to reflect that as well.

The good news here is that you are not your brain generated thoughts, you are not your body, and you are not the world with all of its turmoil. You are the noticer of all of that. Yes, your consciousness/Awareness lives in a body, and that body is subject to all of what's going on in it and around it, but when you've successfully habituated and begun to consistently embody The Real You principles, your ability to simply observe all of it will leave you in a place of power and resilience, not in a place of victimhood. You can develop a new thought undercurrent simply by being more readily aware of its existence and its content, gradually noticing more and more of the fragments floating by that don't work for you, and methodically, mindfully, and consciously replacing the thoughts that don't work for you! Remember the Point A and Point B. Remember the resolve-refine-release process. Do your work and life gets better!

Time to get a little scientific again.

Strings of connected nerve cells, and their connecting dendrites and axons, send signals all through the body and brain. You touch a hot pot on the stove, and the impulse runs through your finger, up your arm to your brain where the, *"OUCH, THAT HURTS!"* message registers quite clearly and loudly. Then, an impulse is immediately sent back down to your finger where the, *"PULL YOUR FINGER BACK AND SHOUT EXPLETIVES,"* message happens soon thereafter. I said, "a little scientific," right? Now to get a little more scientific.

Nerve cells are surrounded by a sleeve known as the myelin sheath. Between the nerve cells and myelin sheath are cells that act as both space fillers and facilitators, known as glial cells. (Albert Einstein is said to have had more glial cells in his brain than pretty much anyone ever.) As we repeatedly participate in any activity—working on a baseball swing, digging out a volleyball slam, dribbling a basketball, reading a book, driving a car, or scrambling eggs while making an omelet—the myelin sheath expands, glial cells multiply, and nerve cell transmission gets both more effective and more efficient. Soon, we have what amounts to a thicker wire carrying more current with less resistance! This process is known as *myelination*. What soon becomes available through this myelination process is that the activity we've been practicing repeatedly (literally) gets easier and requires less energy to perform. In athletics, it's known as "muscle memory," "grooving your golf swing," and "being in the zone." It can also apply to speed reading efficiency, reading comprehension, singing, or any other activity we enjoy and upon which we wish to improve.

Though your brain will perceive both good news and bad news about myelination, by practicing The Real You principles even the challenges presented by myelination are able to be overcome. Know, too, that by simply becoming more aware of your myelinated thought undercurrent, you will dramatically reduce its effect on your daily life and perhaps negate altogether its "charge" on thoughts floating around in the background all day.

CHAPTER TWELVE

EASIER SAID THAN DONE, EASIER DONE THAN BEEN

W e've all heard the first part as an everyday expression. Basically, it means it's easier to talk about doing something than to actually do it. But how about that second part? I'd bet you've never heard that addition until now. It came through for me when I was with one of my counseling clients. What's that second part about?

We can do something that we've promised to do. We can actually get around to that thing we keep saying we'll do. But who will we be being as we're doing it? Who will we be being after we've completed the task? Who we're being is crucial, not only to completing the task but to the quality of the job as it's being accomplished, which will have a significant impact on the quality of the completed task. How we're feeling about the task—before, during, and after its completion—will be so much better! *This is at the essence of mastery,* and this mastery can apply to anything that matters to us!

My mom used to make biscuits from my great-grandmother's recipe. They were and still are the best I've ever tasted. "MuhMah's Biscuits," as we called them, were crumbly, yet fluffy, holding delicately and perfectly together to absorb that scrumptious butter and/or syrup and/or honey that we'd put on them. Those biscuits, when prepared by MuhMah or by Mom, were the best *ever.* We actually felt better after we ate them! There are many family stories that include the heavenly taste of those mouthwatering morsels.

When I made them, however, they just weren't the same. I made sure to use the same ingredients from the same brands and always in the same amounts. I'd do all of the same things Mom and MuhMah did, but they weren't the same biscuits. They looked the same, had the same basic texture, color, etc., and were still pretty darned compliment-worthy, but something was missing. Then I recalled something both my great-grandmother and my mom had casually mentioned as they were making the biscuits.

"Make sure you put a little love in there, too."

The *doingness* had been the same, but the *beingness* wasn't there. When I was being the producer of these delicious morsels of magnificence, pouring love into every step of the process during the measuring and adding of ingredients, feeling the texture and exact degree of stickiness in the dough before rolling them out with some flour and cutting them to shape with the right-sized small juice-glass, when I was really enjoying all the little details, they were better than ever!

Once I began adding a little love to everything I cooked, everything was better! My gumbo recipe was derived from a Mrs. Welch back home, who cooked gumbo for Louisiana's governor when he came to our little town of Opelousas. It was always good gumbo, but was transformed into bowls of culinary ecstasy by loving my way through the preparation of the roux (the flour-and-oil base of any tasty and rich gumbo), adding the seasonings and veggies, adding the water, browning the meat and adding it to the mixture—every step into which I poured in the love, the more "flow" there was to the whole thing, and the better the gumbo kept getting!

Eventually, I added my favorite Cajun music from Nathan and the Zydeco Cha-Chas, Boozoo Chavis, Beau Soleil, and others while I was making my gumbo. It kept getting better! Next thing I knew, I had purchased a commercial-grade, 24-quart stock pot that takes up over half of my stove top, making my gumbo for groups up to fifty, with people clamoring for it and even paying me to make it for parties! What had been missing? I hadn't poured the love into every step of the process! Who I was being was much more important than what I was doing or how I was doing it!

Once I learned this magnificent secret, I began noticing how I felt after going out to eat at various restaurants. Even at fast-food places, the locations where staff was more effectively trained and seemed to be enjoying themselves more were invariably the places where, after eating there, I actually felt better. Years ago, I got a literal as well as figurative taste of this experience when I went out with a dear friend to a modest-looking Chinese restaurant. Even now, thirty years later, the entire experience remains memorable!

On the drive over, my friend told me "This place we're going doesn't look like much, but you're going to love it!" The instant we walked in I felt a light, peaceful presence. Time seemed to be slowing down around us. It was palpable! I looked at my buddy only three steps into the establishment and was about to tell him what I was experiencing, and he just gave me a look of understanding and said "Pretty amazing, right?!" We sat down, ordered, and soon were thoroughly enjoying our impeccably prepared meal. A short while later an older gentleman (maybe in his eighties?) came up to our table and asked how we were enjoying the meal. We told him how delicious the food was and how much we were enjoying the whole experience! He gave us a look and a peaceful smile of appreciation for our appreciation, and the hair on my neck and arms stood up for a few seconds. As he walked away, my friend said, "He's the owner, the chef, and the father or grandfather of almost everyone working here. He was the Master Chef at the finest Chinese restaurant in the city, and after he'd been retired a few years, he opened this place just because he loves it all so much!"

Another one of The Real You principles to apply gratefully to everything you're doing: *Easier said than done. Easier done than been.*

Now let's get a bit esoteric. Consider the possibility that who we're being at any given moment affects everything around us. I'll present more depth on this in a later chapter, but consider that as we more often and more readily touch our own divinity as we Access The Real You, the very energy in the spaces between every subatomic particle of our here-and-now physicality becomes like a beacon within and around us, impacting the divinity in others. Consider the possibility that if we're co creating with Creator, who we're being allows divinity to pour out through us, as us, into everything we do in every moment! That way of being influences everything we're thinking, doing, and experiencing. We're radiating that energy out into the world every single moment of our lives, which you will soon discover can be beautifully infectious! Surely you've noticed that you just feel better being around some people? Trust that you too have ready access to this quality of being, and now you know how to access it!

Before your brain asks the next question, I'll answer it for you. Do I expect you to remain in this state of Present Awareness every moment of every day? Of course not, but it's possible to spend more time in that place of INspiration, INtuition, and ENthusiasm than you do now, with the goal of spending more time there tomorrow than today, and more time there the day after that. We'll have days where it's easier to access and days when it's more challenging to access, and that's fine! "Easier" vs. "harder" and "yesterday vs. today vs. tomorrow vs. the next day" are nothing more than another "Point A vs. Point B" brain-generated comparison. It's just the brain doing its job. But you are not your brain, you are the noticer of it!

CHAPTER THIRTEEN

AND WHAT OF THE BODY WHICH HOUSES THE REAL YOU?

Like it or not, as much as we now know that you're not your brain generating thought, or the body with a brain that's pumping out the thoughts, we must remember that The Real You is blessed to occupy physical space as the body in which we play and create, through which we deeply feel emotions throughout that body, and through which continuity and flow may occur and be experienced. Given the inexorable connection between the mind, soul, and body, what's happening to us is, on some esoteric level due, at least in part, to what we're carrying on a soulful and emotional level. This in turn informs brain activity, whether we want it to or not, and in the opposite direction as well—brain to body and body to brain. What I learned by noticing my brain's musings as The Real You that I am is that these principles are intended to be applied to my entire body, not just to my brain, and also to the world around me as I'm experiencing it (more on that third part in later chapters).

While noticing my thoughts, I noticed I was experiencing discomfort or even outright pain in specific parts of my body when the "thought undercurrent" mentioned earlier was impacting most heavily and occupying most disconcertingly a certain part of my body. I noticed too that I could see how symbolically and, in fact, literally connected the thoughts were with the body part affected!

For example, when my bank account got below a certain amount, I'd have lower back pain, even though a top-notch chiropractor had supported my complete healing in that area. When my younger son would be his typical-middle-school self—becoming a frustration, usually on purpose, and taking me away from work I needed to do—what was I to do, not be his dad? I found sometimes that as much as I totally loved my son, taking care of him made it feel that my being a good father was literally preventing me from "walking my walk" with regard to earning a better living and providing for him as best I could (and that aspect of fatherhood has always been an issue until I applied The Real You principles to it). At such times, my left knee would ache to the point of impeding my walk!

Would you venture a guess where body ache about his mom was located? Yep; she was quite literally the pain in my neck!

Want to know the only solution that's turned out to be the solution to all of these? Love, darn it! A love bigger than all of the waste material generated by my brain about every life aspect one could mention. From my deepest misery and biggest challenges, I learned the art of what I call "spiritual composting." If you're familiar with composting, spiritual composting is no different than regular composting. In real-world composting, you take some food or animal fecal matter, then add leaves, nonmeat and nonoily food, and some grass clippings. Add these in proper ratios, turn it every few days, and then let Creator, mycelium, and time transform this bunch of mess into the richest and healthiest material you can put on your garden!

Can we do the same with the thoughts of our experiences that affect our minds and bodies? Yes, we can! We can take the fecal matter of our lives (whatever is wearing you down and wearing you out); add a little perspective gained from noticing the Point As and Point Bs in our lives; noticing and learning why those Point Bs are Point Bs for us; resolving, refining, and releasing; and turn whatever mess we've created in our lives into a life-compost-rich environment in which to live and continue learning from this time forward.

You can do this! It takes time, but you have the rest of your life in which to master it. Every aspect of your life you can notice from The

Real You place can be improved upon! The more you myelinate that new way, the better at it you will become, and the more each and every aspect of your life—especially the ones to which the brain most predictably defaults into the present-day troublesome rabbit hole—soon defaults into your new and better way!

Noticing the thoughts that preceded my own physical aches and pains showed me how these two seemingly disparate parts of me were in fact intimately connected. Like it or not, on some very concrete level, all physical ailments have a spiritual, emotional, and brain-generated cause, and this is what we will experience, if not remedied, as dis-ease.

I heard a truly remarkable real-life story of this on an old podcast a while back, where people in the area of Nepal/Tibet/Bhutan were being interviewed because there was an extraordinary amount of people living there who claimed to be in their 130s, 140s, 150s, and even 160s! Naturally, the film crew wanted to document these people's diet, exercise regimen, and every recordable aspect of their lives to determine a possible pattern they could bring back and share with the modern Western world. Through a translator, everyone interviewed had the same basic response. What was their secret to such long life? They all said, basically, "If you don't learn how to let things go in your life (the troublesome, tedious, frustrating, and saddening aspects we all encounter), you just can't live past 90 or so. If, however, you can learn how to work through the things you can work through, and let the rest go, you can live decades longer, as we do."

Point A and Point B! Notice why your Point Bs are Point Bs for you, study them for what they have to teach you about yourself, then practice resolve-refine-release! Simple, yet not easy again, right? Remember, too, that "easy" is just a brain-generated comparison! This work never ends but, as the people in this remote and remarkable village have learned and practice daily in their lives, incredible things become possible when we practice The Real You principles.

Our bodies are reflections of what's happening inside us. Remember that place where Jesus said Heaven lies? Within us! We are vibrational beings who *are* awareness. When we learn to more readily stand in

99

that place beyond conditional happiness, conditional self-worth, and conditional security, there's just not much that can shake us off that peaceful foundation.

Care of and for the body is crucial since it's where The Real You resides. Of course, it's not a requirement per se, but giving it what it needs to stay strong and healthy means eating healthy food, drinking lots of good water, breathing good air, and keeping your brain chatter at bay with The Real You's awareness.

Here's where we get a bit more esoteric again, or so it may seem if you're one of those folks who's spent your whole life following the Western medical model of "attack a symptom" rather than "discover the underlying cause of the disease," which will more positively and directly impact the condition. Thousands of years ago, there was a culture that learned what we now call "The Chakra System." Interestingly enough, thousands of years later and thousands of miles away, the ancient Hebrew Gnostics were receiving their equivalent book known as the Kabbalah. I find it fascinating that the same concepts of energy centers are described and correlated to the same life aspects, ways of being, things to notice, and remedies that may be applied. The bottom line here is that who we are being about any given issue will, if we are carrying conflicting/heavy/discordant energy about that issue, give rise to emotional upset, and eventually give rise as well to physical symptoms that may be alleviated by applying wisdom, discernment, and taking appropriate actions (applying The Real You principles).

Better food, better air, and better water will yield a healthier and stronger body, as well as a more effective immune response to disease. Never forget that any disease starts inside us, often as a result of a weakened immune state, which in turn is often caused by not practicing The Real You principles, which leads to accumulated stressors that can wear us down and out.

It sounds so obvious, but we don't always give our bodies what they need. I'm no doctor, but I can say with authority that drinking lots of good water (I've been told we're 80 percent water, and I'm told that 70 percent of that water resides in the lymphatic system, which benefits greatly when we move our bodies around on a regular basis, so . . .), getting a fair amount of exercise and a good night's sleep all make a positive impact on your health.

Moving your body

I've always been into sports, but as I've gotten older, I've found some are harder to do. I can still throw, catch, and punt a football, but I'm not playing tackle football any longer. There are still those in which I participate, but there are two movement practices that are for anyone, regardless of age, and even of ability to move around: yoga and Pilates. Yoga has been around for thousands of years, and I must admit it does an amazing job of supporting strength, flexibility, and mindfulness about one's body. If you're new to yoga, I'd bet there's a beginner's class somewhere nearby and some available online as well. I recommend in-person instruction at first (you may need to apply The Real You principles to get past the natural uneasiness and perhaps self-consciousness of being a beginner) to make sure your body is in the proper positioning, so you can feel into what "correct" is for you. The more you practice, the easier it gets, the more flexible you'll be, and the stronger your body will become, surprisingly so, in fact, in my experience!

Yoga and/or other movement practice is a wonderful support for body, mind, and spirit. In moving your body around, you may find places that are sore, stiff, or weakened. Yoga is a wonderful way to discern those places, to breathe energy into them, and to breathe out what's in the way of improved health, strength, and flexibility. Science is now showing that we are nothing more than energy slowed down into the realm of perceivable physical bandwidth, so becoming more aware of the energy, which not only comprises us but also supports us, is essential. From The Real You place, you can intuit what's needed and, with good yoga instruction, implement it.

Same with Pilates. Though not an ancient practice, it's profoundly effective! Pilates is as good as anything I've known for learning where your body-center-balance line is and why that's important (more than I'd ever have realized). It is also superb for strengthening your body. Pilates uses weights, your own body weight, and your own body momentum, to enhance strength and flexibility by engaging the various apparatus and going back and forth among them. Again, if you're new (I'd certainly still classify myself very much a novice beginner), find a friendly and supportive instructor, and it will carry you far!

Making up your own movement program can work, too! Sometimes, when I'm really in flow and just Being in the moment, I'll step back from a recurring and persistent physical ailment, and sometimes (not always, if I'm stuck in my preferences about it going away) I'll remember to ask Spirit for a solution, and it works! A while back, my right shoulder got extremely stiff and sore. I tried stretching it up, down, back and forth, and nothing seemed to help. I breathed into it in my ultra-basic yoga practice, and this didn't do much better. I meditated on my shoulder, peering deeply into the structure of the joint, and suddenly I got a vision of me swinging my arm in a big circle, a bit like The Who's Pete Townshend wailing away on his guitar in that same series of huge circles. I was apprehensive, since I'd not even been able to raise my arm up from my side higher than ear-level, but I tried it and, amazingly, when I was swinging my arm in a full circle, holding nothing back, free of caution or concern, not only were my arm and shoulder able to accommodate this movement and speed, but after only seven or eight of these high-speed revolutions, my shoulder pain and limited movement completely vanished! The point is that what I thought to be true had been true until I intuited, from The Real You place, something completely different, which then yielded a result I'd never have considered possible.

Food

I'm not a doctor, and I'm not a nutritionist, but I can tell you what works for me, and I strongly recommend you dig into it and discover for yourself what works for you.

I've never been one to diet, but I've always found that when I eat healthy food my cravings for unhealthy products decrease dramatically! I have a big salad almost every day, filled with items providing a variety of colors. It's pretty and provides a healthy variety of nutrients. Lettuce, cucumbers, tomatoes, yellow and orange bell peppers, and celery all make their way into my salads on a regular basis. Salad works wonders for getting enough fiber to keep our insides clean, as well as providing a lot of vitamins and minerals our bodies need. I make my own salad dressings with a variety of spices; no additives or preservatives whenever I can manage it. I steam veggies on a regular basis too, which, when not over-steamed—just enough to soften them a bit and bring out a vibrant color—preserves nutritional value as well as the great flavor! I have no problem with real butter and consider it far better than those "healthy" fake-butter spreads that are often packed with artificial goo I prefer to avoid. Interestingly, veggies and fruits are not only very healthy, they're also far less expensive than junk food.

Years ago, someone told me, "The closer it is to the way God made it, the better it is for you!" I have friends who've transformed their weakened cardiovascular systems and impaired digestive tracts by going vegan and even raw vegan. Not my thing, but I've seen it work miracles, without lots of chemical medicines and man-made stuff that Big Pharma prefers we ingest. Mother Nature really has provided us with a plethora of wonderful options that are all readily available, very affordable, and tasty! I strongly recommend reading and learning, trying new things, and finding out what works for you in the way that's uniquely your own! Again, I'll never say "stop taking your doctor-prescribed medication," but I will use the old expression "an ounce of prevention is worth a pound of cure."

In colder months, I enjoy soups filled with veggies and occasionally some meat (and gazpacho in summer) and find that making big batches to cook and freeze is a great time-saver. Being a Cajun, I make gigantic batches of chicken and sausage gumbo a few times each winter—olive oil instead of lard, nitrite-free sausage, healthy chicken, and I skim off the oil and excess fat after cooking it down for several hours. I also love pasta—fettucine alfredo, to which I add grilled veggies like yellow and zucchini squash, onions, and minced garlic, as well as various pastas with my own homemade spaghetti sauce, which is really quite easy once you find a recipe you like. The best part of cooking, when I have time, is experimenting. Never be afraid to make a mistake. Mistakes are usually still edible, and a lesson learned with self-love and self-forgiveness (remember the Real You principles!) is a lesson remembered.

I enjoy fruit and pretty much any fruit. Bananas and apples, kiwis, mangos and pineapples (in moderation for me because of the high acid content), and a wide variety of berries—strawberries, blueberries (rich in antioxidants), and fresh picked blackberries—as well as oranges, lemons, limes, grapes, raisins, prunes, and melons of all types. Then there are nuts and seeds—pecans, peanuts, cashews, macadamias, pine nuts, and sunflower seeds among others. All are so very tasty, healthy, and fun to mix and match and drop into everything from breakfast cereal to a lunch or dinner salad, or even cooked up and served as dessert. Remember (again, I'm not a doctor), that most plant-based oils are actually pretty healthy in moderation, so olives, nuts, and other plant-based oil-rich foods are usually fine.

I eat meat, but have consumed far less beef and more chicken, nitrite-free pork loins, and quality seafood over the last several years. I love to bake or grill a full-sized salmon filet with a little lemon juice and tarragon, and never overcook it, so the wonderful omegas are there to enjoy! I have found playing with herbs and spices to be so much fun. Feeling uncomfortable with choosing herbs and spices for your meal? Here's a tip for you: smell the food, then smell the herb/spice. If it feels like a match, go for it! Second tip: Go easy on the herbs and spices until you know how much you like. The idea is to enhance the taste of the item seasoned, not to overcome it.

I still love my dairy, though no milk—usually almond milk for me, though I still love my high-quality ice cream, Greek yogurt with fruit that I add myself—bananas, strawberries, and blueberries are my favorites—and I adore cheese, in moderation.

I enjoy high-quality supplements as well, knowing that I never seem to get enough vitamins and minerals in my chosen foods. A doctor friend recommended CoQ10 ages ago, because he said our factory-farmed, generally-depleted soil lacks this essential nutrient. I take a multivitamin twice a day, which sounds like double what's needed. But when I was advised to check the minimum daily requirements from other countries, I found that what our FDA considers healthy is considered insufficient in other countries. I choose more over less nutritional content in my food intake. I was told by a nurse many years ago that 5000 IU of Vitamin D3 would help keep me healthy, and aside from getting COVID-19, I haven't been sick more than once every few years since (and my doctor told me that my consistent Vitamin D3 intake likely saved my life). Also included in my diet is fish oil rich in omegas, Vitamin E, a diverse probiotic (which I've found is why I can enjoy high-quality ice cream again!), and 1000 to 2000 mg of Vitamin C. Again, I'm not a nutritionist and am only mentioning what I ingest. Check with your medical or holistic professional for the best individualized advice for you!

CHAPTER FOURTEEN

APPLYING THE REAL YOU PRINCIPLES TO YOUR LIFE AS IT OCCURS AROUND YOU

Remember the magician's magic tricks? They're not magic, though it might look that way when the spontaneity of the moment outpaces the brain's ability to generate the usual "what's likely to be next" scenario. These are the moments when "flow" is happening, and the way to get there is by noticing what is not flow and then not judge it. Just make the time to drop into, for even a few moments, The Real You Place and savor as valuable even the most challenging circumstances for the teaching content they may provide for you.

It is in those times that our brains so often require, or perhaps desperately hope for, some semblance of order and at least some level of certainty. When things seem out of balance, please take notice of the cycles of your life. In the never-ending cycles expressed in our physical reality, we may enjoy the peace that comes over us as we witness the ocean waves coming in and out. We can notice peacefully as our lungs breathe in and out. Come to know the cycles of your life at whatever level you're able to perceive them around you at any given time (again, without judgment), just being with what arises and falls away. Jobs or projects at work starting and ending, club and other memberships coming and going, romantic relationships that may only be a season, but from which we may learn and grow—all seen from a higher, zoomed-out perspective as cycles to be noticed and kept within a broader, longer-term perspective. There are always challenging times, but when we can embrace them as nothing more than that—times that for now represent difficulties to get through and from which we learn—even the most excruciating moments can be noticed and remembered as valuable.

Music has upbeats and downbeats, and slower and faster pacing within a composition. We can witness and even see from satellites the air currents surrounding and breathing our Mother Earth. We are able to see sine waves—the beautiful variable waveforms that are by an understanding of physics and engineering made measurable and visible, which in turn may be applied to electrical waveforms, radio waves, and waves of air, all cyclical in nature and about which we may peacefully pause and wonder.

Remember, too, that you are, at your Divine Essence, one with All that Is. You may not be God, as it were, but your Divine Nature contains within it the fullness of the Nature of The Divine. When life mirrors back to you someone saying, "Great job!" or you get a clear sign of "yes!" to what you're doing, acknowledge these experiences as your cocreation with Creator! It all happens for a reason, and You . . . Are . . . It. Remember to hold the felt intention of that which you are seeking, and trust that every step of the way is one step closer to your goals. If that's the space you're holding—empty space filled with possibility, and not space filled with your expectations and preferences—then everything that occurs along your way is exactly what's supposed to happen, even if it doesn't look the way your brain thinks it should. Your thinking—the brain's ongoing, instantly-applied judgments and comparisons of what occurs to what you expect—is always in the way if that's where your focus is directed.

When you're holding truly empty space filled with possibility, while holding your dreams and expectations outside the space of life's occurrences, you can watch with eager anticipation every moment's manifestation, recognizing it all as progression toward your goals. Remember that in noticing what's occurring and how you're being about it all, you free yourself from the burdensome judgments, preferences, and expectations you might otherwise actively carry into that space of life's present moments, simply by leaving them in the background. You can make your vision boards, write your affirmations, etc., but don't burden yourself by holding on to them, comparing every experience as "aligned with" or "not aligned with" your preferred experience. Make your plan, hold on to the "what," and release the where/when/why/how to universal flow. Sometimes life won't occur as you planned, but it is still heading in the direction required in the etheric realm of consciousness that will lead to the manifestation you seek—again, perhaps not exactly as you'd anticipated. But please trust the process. Follow the instructions of your Knowing. If you're not clear and not hearing that Divine Knowing, you may sometimes be better off doing nothing than taking steps that take you farther off center. Many years ago, a wise man told me, as I was seeking clarity about some important personal matters, "Spirit may not always show you green lights, but It will always show you red ones." I've found this extremely useful when my brain chatter gets me bogged down and starts to overcome momentum I've built up. If it's a "No," I always see that (though I may not pay attention to what I've heard), and when I don't get a "green light," I keep going if I'm not sensing clearly a "red light." For the record, when I didn't get a red light, and painful things happened, I still grew and evolved from the experience in ways that would never have happened if I'd not walked forward trusting in the process. Somehow, in a place beyond my thinking, I intuited a path that, though challenging, was very well worth it!

Notice your possibly beneath-conscious thoughts that are dualistic "judgments": good/bad, easy/hard, soon/later, early/late, short time/long time. Even if not a "negative," per se, these are still dualistic, which is a demonstration of the brain's having generated these thoughts. The more you notice that you can notice, the greater the extent to which you will most surely become the master of them. Even if you can't stop the thoughts, your very awareness will shift you from being controlled to being the controller, regardless of the intensity and quantity of your brain's thoughts! You can have anger and even express it in a controlled way, without it having you!

Here's the next piece of this: The intensity of any given thought, who you're being about it, and how you might be judging a person, feeling, or experience may itself be grounded in your preference and perception about the person, feeling, or experience. Your experience of a car salesperson, for example, can be as much or more based on who you're being about car salespeople in general, before ever arriving on the dealer's lot, or who you're being about your finances before ever arriving on the dealer's lot, or what you may have read about the brand or model or color or style or dealership that may have influenced you in some way before you even arrive there. See where this is headed? It's in your brain and body, and it's all around you! But The Real You is not your brain, body, or circumstances, It is the noticer of them!

Another example of preference-influenced reality, Example 1: Someone asks me who I'm rooting for as a possible matchup in the Super Bowl two years from now. I could care less! Not exactly an urgent thing for me, and I certainly don't have a big charge around it or find it worth taking up mind space with. If one of my few favorite teams isn't in, who cares; and we're not even talking about this year's Super Bowl! Too far away, no intensity, and no big deal.

Example 2: Someone wants me to deliver The Real You principles to help motivate and focus each of the football teams that will be participating in next year's Super Bowl. Now I'm interested! Who's playing? Who cares! I AM IN!

Once again, it's not about what's happening but about who you're being about what's happening, and suddenly my whole notion about next year's Super Bowl has amped up! Suddenly, I'm looking up the dates of the game, reaching out to the TV network about how many people and in what room I'll be delivering the talk, where the game and talk will happen, hotel reservations, etc. Completely different experience based on how much I care! Loads of intensity now, so it's a big deal!

The more you can notice what's happening around you and who you're being about it all, the more your life's experiences can teach you. Even the most mundane of moments may prove useful when you're standing in The Real You place, open to insights available there.

CHAPTER FIFTEEN

OVERCOMING HARMFUL HABITS AND ATTITUDES—MYELINATION—WHY IT'S HARD, AND WHY YOU CAN DO IT!

M yelination is the process by which, through repeated stimulation of a nerve-pathway during a given activity, the myelin sheath surrounding nerve cells (with glial cells in between) is developed and enhanced. This results in increased effectiveness and efficiency in that nervous system pathway's energetic transmission. Basically, what happens when we do something repeatedly and systematically over time is that the myelin sheath expands, glial cells multiply, and the nerve cells inside actually transmit more energy with less effort. It literally behaves like a thicker wire carrying more current with less resistance! In other words, if you practice proper form on your tennis forehand, and do the stroke hundreds of times, what some would call "muscle memory" or "being in the zone" starts to take over, and it literally becomes easier to hit a proper stroke and requires less energy to do so!

The good news is that any activity can be myelinated—reading speed and comprehension, chess play, playing a musical instrument, or driving a car. Remember, too, that thoughts are nothing more than combinations of brain cells flashing together, so thoughts can get myelinated as well. Thus, if we keep the good thoughts flowing it gets easier and takes less energy to think positive thoughts, maintain a positive outlook, see positive results, feel positive feelings more readily, and be more resilient amid challenges!

The bad news, for all the same reasons, is that if we think sad thoughts, depressing thoughts, or frightened thoughts, these can also become myelinated. I believe this is at the root of chronic depression, deeply rooted trauma reaction, and the like. I won't attempt to argue with an MD/psychiatrist about which came first, the chicken or the egg, but I'm clear that once such thoughts are myelinated, it not only takes less effort in less time for depressed thoughts to arise and take hold, it can become harder to pull ourselves out of it.

More good news, however: In my healing practice, I've had a few clients who were on their "depression cocktail" for decades, and yet, by implementing The Real You principles, were slowly but surely able to wean themselves off of one, then two, then the rest of their medications. PLEASE NOTE THAT I AM NOT A DOCTOR. I AM NOT RECOMMENDING THAT ANYONE STOP TAKING THEIR DOCTOR-PRESCRIBED MEDICATION(S). I'M NOT SAYING THAT THIS "WEANING OFF" PROCESS IS RECOMMENDED WITHOUT MEDICAL SUPERVISION, NOR AM I SAYING IT WILL WORK FOR EVERYONE. But I am most definitely asserting that it is very much possible to myelinate new thought-sequences, thought-processes, and resulting bodily responses that can and have supported people in freeing themselves of chemical dependencies.

Even in the midst of deep sadness, happiness can be cultivated, as we shift from anger to peace, frustration to satisfaction, fear to calm, and paranoia to pronoia. We can develop, over time, the proverbial rope to pull us out of even the deepest rut. We can notice a myelinated regret that lives in a no-longer-now past and transform it into a powerful teaching moment through our structured application of Real You principles. Our Present, in which new activities and ways of being may be created and practiced, and into which we may become grounded, is thus able to be enhanced. The myelinated stress of the present moment may be reduced and eventually eliminated by new myelinated thoughts and ways of being grounded in acceptance and trust in our ongoing growth and expansion, so that new and more productive outcomes may gradually become more readily and confidently expected to occur.

Likewise with thoughts of worry: Thought patterns grounded in a future that has yet to occur or are based in a time long past, may now be replaced with new possibilities for a better future! By practicing The Real You principles, we can identify issues, we can apply the Point A—Point B learning process to them, and then resolve-refine-release the issues so we can be empowered to step faithfully forward into an uncertain future, armed with the self-trust, self-confidence, self-forgiveness, and self-love required to tackle any obstacle real or imagined.

The freedom that becomes available appears truly magical and miraculous, but it's not magic, and it's not a miracle. One of my heroes, Gregg Braden, said, "The difference between a miracle and technology is an explanation." The Real You principles are the explanation and, therefore, the technology that makes it possible when you diligently practice applying them.

But when will that be? What is required? How can it be done? Who/what inside you requires the answer to that question? Any hint of where/when/by when/why/how/how long, and any comparison of "this and that," or other "need to know with certainty" is your instant clue that you're in brain chatter and not in The Real You place. If your brain is insisting on knowing "how long," here's the answer to how long myelination takes: twenty-one days. Ever heard, "It takes twenty-one days to form a new habit"? I'm told that this is how long myelination takes to occur completely. Keep in mind that we're not talking about, "I practiced every few days for a few minutes for twenty-one days." We're talking about diligently practicing for twenty-one days, and then watching what happens when you do! Once you're grounded in The Real You principles and practice these simple-but-not-always-easy exercises, you will achieve results. Learn to trust in and become comfortable with how that knowing feels and occurs in your body. Where the brain will always require "certainty," The Real You sits in stillness, Knowing, and a peace that brains can't begin to figure out or understand.

We can free ourselves of depression, and we can myelinate our own new and more effective habitual thought undercurrents of love, of calm amid any storm, and of motivated and inspired action. We can myelinate a new thought undercurrent of beauty and confidence. How nice will it be to have this new thought undercurrent always running in the background instead of an undercurrent of dread and, "When's the other shoe going to fall?" This new way of being works its way more and more deeply into our unconscious, which Carl Jung said is the part of us that creates and manifests!

Want to know how big a superpower controlling our unconscious thoughts can be? I heard Dr. Bruce Lipton tell a story of starting a phone call in his car about five minutes in to a thirty-minute drive. The call ended as he entered the parking lot of his destination, and he realized that he'd driven the last twenty miles paying no conscious attention whatsoever to his driving or his route. The subconscious/unconscious parts of our brains are quite powerful and quite capable indeed! Ever watched a professional athlete "in the zone," or a timed game of speed chess? Flow is literally that! All we have to do is just be, and the flow will carry us forward without our having to push through it all!

Here's the bottom line: Every day you're not practicing The Real You principles is another day of living with the burden of accumulating negative thoughts and resulting brain chemistry and bodily disease. I just heard on the radio that 100 million people in the United States have high-blood pressure. That's 30 percent of the population of the entire country! Ready to be part of the healthier side of that percentage? Practice! Start now!

CHAPTER SIXTEEN

APPLYING THE REAL YOU PRINCIPLES TO RELATIONSHIPS WITH FRIENDS, FAMILY MEMBERS, AND EVERYONE

Friends and family members are those people about whom we generally hold the strongest preferences, desires, and expectations for possible outcomes. How often have you found yourself upset at "what was said vs. what you thought was said"? or, "what was said vs. what you'd wish was said instead"? or "what was done or done to you vs. what you thought about it, especially if it directly or indirectly applies to something you did or said, or something based in who you are"? Exhausting, right?

Friends and family are special when it's all about loving each other unconditionally and supporting each other in what we're up to. Stop and consider those relationships that you find not just enjoyable but empowering and inspiring.

Who are these people? Why are they special to you? When are they or were they special to you? Was there an added importance around the timing of the relationship? Where were you—physically, mentally, emotionally, and spiritually—at the time of your coming together and remaining together? How did they affect you? How does your relationship with them affect you now? All of these factors, and so many more, affect our feelings, preferences, and expectations about those most important people in our lives.

Consider, too, a future filled with your most cherished people around you. Do you carry concerns, worries, or outright dread about future encounters with certain friends or family members? Stop and consider: First, what are your concerns? How many of these may be improved upon by applying The Real You principles? After doing some Point A—Point B practice on these, why are they concerns for you? Can you apply the resolve-refine-release practice to these concerns? How are these affecting you now, and how might it look and feel to see these concern-areas improved upon within you and about the people involved? What might life look and feel like with these concerns eliminated? Start envisioning that! Start feeling what that would feel like! Swim around in those thoughts!

I challenge you to practice The Real You principles around all of your relationships. The most challenging applications of The Real You principles will always be regarding friends and family precisely *because* they're friends and family! Remember, "It always hurts exactly as much as you care"? The flipside of that also applies: "It always excites and enlivens exactly as much as you care!" If you're a parent, aunt, or uncle, how great does it feel to see your loved one excel at a sport or win an academic award in school, or even learn to walk, read, or ride a bicycle?

Awareness and practice will always improve your attitude, focus, and power. Being the noticer makes you invincible with practice. Will it change the people and circumstances? Perhaps so, perhaps not, but I promise you that *you* will feel better once you've learned how to distance yourself from your brain chatter and ground yourself in The Real You place. How people and circumstances occur may pleasantly surprise you when The Real You principles are practiced diligently. Again, this may be a somewhat esoteric notion, but expect life to actually occur differently when you're in this place!

Consider your present moment. How are present-moment thoughts about people and circumstances affecting you now? What's actually happening? Who's it actually happening to? Is it happening to me? Is it happening to others? Does it actually affect me? What is the subjective perception vs. objective reality of the situation, and can we even know the difference in the moment? Why is it happening? Keep in mind the extent to which our reality is shaped by our expectations and preferences. Where is it happening? Does the location hold any special significance for me? Are memories and/or emotions evoked by the very location itself?

What are you willing to share with those around you about your present moment? Consider the present moment as the culmination of your life up to now. What got you here? Can you discern any experiences that lead you to other experiences or moments that have impacted who and how you are at this moment? Who are you now because of these experiences? Are there experiences or people in your life history that are hard for you to speak about or even think about now without a noticeable charge around them? Why is that? When did these happen? What was happening in your life and in your mind at that time that made the person, experience, or situation what it was?

I know that just reading these questions can activate bioenergetically various body parts, brain chatter, and removing the cover to that rabbit hole into which you've previously fallen. Are you finding yourself, in simply remembering the crisis, descending down that rabbit hole, shifting from self-examination and Presence to experiencing the thoughts, and feeling the emotions during the challenges of that time? Stop and breathe in to five and out to eight, four times. Smile a big smile, even if you have to force it.

Remember that these activate a body-wide relaxation response through the vagus nerve, which touches all major organs in the body. Step back from the situation and notice it all. Notice who and how you were being then, and who and how you're being about it now. Stand in the Awareness that you are; courageously willing to notice and rise above it all, not to "overcome" it, or to in any way attempt to change the people involved, or what happened with them. Simply stand in The Real You place, and know that you are, at your essential level, bigger than any people or circumstances you've ever experienced. Stand tall in love and self-love, forgiveness and self-forgiveness. It's not about overcoming as much as standing in a place above it all, and making that your new way.

Here's the best news about all of it: none of it matters in the NOW! Please remember that it's never been about what happened, or with whom it happened, or where or when or why it happened (though each of these aspects may lend some added perspective to study and from which we may learn). What matters now is noticing who you've been being about it and who you're being about it all *now!*

Remember that all we ever have is this now moment. All of the "now moments" in our past and all of the now moments of our future are beyond time and space; they are all a part of how we experience our "Now moment NOW." You can, by zooming out, be one with it all. You can be The Real You, present to it all and above and beyond it all.

Say out loud, "I've been me through it all. I can now be Most Me and will always be Most Me as life continues to occur, regardless of how it occurs!"

Being fully Present is only possible when you are free of those otherwise-carried-in-the-moment thoughts and feelings about the people and situations that, by definition, prevent that sense of presence and perspective. You must stand in The Real You place. Nowhere to run. Nowhere to hide. No need to run or hide because in that place there is only stillness, peace, and love for yourself and those around you in that "peace that passes understanding." No time and no need for excuses or judgments or regrets or worries.

There's a verse somewhere in the Bible that says, "Be still and know I am God." Years ago when I gathered with a faith community, we would recite a prayer that went like this:

Be still and know I am God.

Be still and know I am.

Be still and know I.

Be still and know.

Be still and.

Be still.

Be.

By the time we'd finished this recitation, the whole room would become completely calmed. There was both a physical and spiritual stillness that moved everyone in the room. The only physical experience was the hair standing up on our arms and on the backs of our necks.

In this level of stillness and connection to the divine within us, so much wisdom, power, and patience become available to us. Also, the level of Divine Connection with others becomes so much more powerful, enlightening, and occasionally, challenging! We must do all we can to stay in that grounded, nonreactive Presence available in The Real You place, especially when our history, wounds, and "triggers" occur. Someone may say a simple word or phrase, or speak something with a particular tone, or even show us an expression that reminds us, consciously or subconsciously, of some person or event in our past. The sooner we can catch ourselves shifting from reaction to response, the better we will be at managing who we're being in our most cherished relationships.

Like sunglasses blocking the light, the filter we are being at any given time can become clouded by the never-ending cacophony in our brains and the free-flowing thought undercurrent. By simply noticing this, we are more readily able to make available to ourselves the wisdom that awaits us. Please do not hear this as so many organized religions that have, in my opinion, twisted and perverted this process. This is not about "doing a thing and getting rewarded with a thing." This is not about proving to someone else that you're valid because you "get it" in some prescriptive way that they say you should, and that if you don't get it in the way they prescribe you're not really a valid member of that group.

It's not as if God/Spirit/Creator is some soda or food dispenser. This is all about you, for you, in the very individualized way that is all your own. What your brain is generating for you to notice, what your body is presenting for you to notice, and what your life is showing you by what's occurring around you—all are there for you to notice in the way that is yours and for you alone. To make this clear, please read the following rather long sentence as many times as it takes for you to Know it down deep into your bones:

The Real You principles are there to guide you in the way that is yours, through noticing and learning what occurs in your brain, in your body, and around you, and the lessons made available to you in The Real You place, which, though universal in their applicability, are yours and yours alone to teach you the lessons that you are here to learn in the way that is yours. This book is not for you to follow like some new Bible. The writings herein are meant to awaken in you your own noticing so you can walk your own walk in the way that your own brain, body, and life's occurrences are making available to you right here, right now! This book is not the way. It is merely a lamp unto your feet, designed to illuminate your path so that you can see the next right step for yourself.

There's a passage attributed, I think, to Jesus, where he said, "Where the heart is, there your treasure lies also." I believe he was referring to that place known by Gnostics around the world throughout history, where we experience for ourselves the treasured peace and joy and fulfillment that become available when we spend more time in The Real You place. There's a flip side to this passage, of course, which may perhaps be implied, but I've never heard spoken, which is, "Where the heart is, there your $#!+ lies also." This is why "fake it 'til you make it" never works in the long run. You can emptily speak thousands of positive affirmations all day and all night for years and still not achieve the result you're seeking. Why is that? Because just speaking something over and over may not be able to overcome the thought undercurrent on which the positive affirmations are floating, preventing anything you don't really believe from sinking in! You must Know the truth of which you're speaking, or it will ring hollow. You must know that you know what you're affirming for yourself is, in fact, your truth and not just something you're saying to help you feel better in any given moment. You must know the truth of yourself down into your bones and into the depths of your soul if you are to manifest the life you say you want.

On Contemporary Societal Polarization

Now that you've had some time to consider all of this with some breadth and depth, you may find that there are many aspects of your life that even after all of your hard work remain unresolved. Most of these, I find, sometimes lie legitimately out of our control. You can't control, for example, how anyone feels about you at any given moment. Refine who you're being about those things you can't resolve, and if anything remains after that, let it go!

Given the ever-more-extreme polarity in American political culture, applying The Real You principles will come in very handy, if not life transforming, wherever they're implemented.

Likewise, the religious messiness in American culture. Spiritual practice is deeply rooted in most cultures around the world. I believe it is in our human nature to unearth and come to know that which sources our Being, for example, and to explore what forces are at work in the never-ending interplay of consciousness expressed in animals, plants, and minerals manifesting into physical existence, and then moving on to whatever energetic and material state is next for them. The more one notices human existence, the lives of pets and other animals both wild and domesticated, the lives of plants, and how every living and nonliving thing has its own version of birth, life, and death, as it were, the more wondrous it all becomes. No matter the breadth and depth of one's store of information, there are still unanswerable, unresolvable questions. Even the greatest minds of science were often, at their best, only able to generate theories, not laws, and postulates that were not always proofs.

Religion as differentiated from spirituality includes "membership" to that religion, and that membership connotes ties between congregants and a leader, as well as between congregants themselves, and between naturally occurring subgroups of congregants. Given the naturally divisive nature of the brain, there are often conflicts that arise between the subgroups and between these groups and ministerial staff, etc. Wherever there are humans, there are conflicts it seems, and because our beliefs about some Supreme Being and our beliefs about our fellow humans are among the most important aspects of most people's lives, nerves get sensitive, hearing gets filtered, tongues get sharpened, and soon there are discussions, then heated discussions, then arguments, then perhaps divisions and even official schisms!

Before things get out of hand here, are you willing to step back enough in the moment to love and forgive and grant space to others when they've fallen into their pit of brain-generated burning rage and righteous indignation, unconscious of The Real You place of which you're now aware? Are you willing to love and forgive yourself, forgiving and granting space to yourself when you find yourself diving down the rabbit hole of your own justifications for your anger, frustration, disappointment, and pain—all of which are a reaction to differences and not a response toward a desired mutual understanding, evolution, accommodation, and unification?

Don't be ashamed if you're finding it a huge challenge to accomplish this new way of being around these matters. Historically, there are broad-based labels like Judaism, Christianity, Islam, Hinduism, Buddhism, and many others, within which are many denominations, sects, and other officially- and unofficially-recognized segments whose members often prefer to be perceived as differentiated. Judaism, for example, is comprised of reform, reconstructionist, conservative, and orthodox, and within each of these are many variations. Regarding Jesus-followers, there are over fifteen hundred Protestant Christian denominations in the United States alone, along with multiple segments of the Catholic church, the "Jews for Jesus" movement, and so many more!

What is one thing that all of these have in common? Each one of its practitioners often believes themselves to be right and others to be wrong, if not absolutely, to at least some degree. When that how-much-you-care intensity level is very high, as is usually the case around such heart-felt and brain-screaming matters, things can get intense!

I'm not trying to be too hard on religious practice. Religious gatherings offer people a place to feel acceptance and belonging, as well as the provision of a place in which one may contribute and be validated for their service to something greater than themselves. When one receives such validation, the importance of that gathering place and one's mental/emotional mindset about that place becomes enormous. Some people can get into a prideful place and might exclaim, "My place is better than yours because it feels that way to *me,* and I'm right to feel that way because I believe it is so, and if you disagree, *you're* the problem." Many feel this way about their house of worship and that their membership, while not exclusive, can and often does begin to stimulate an egotistic need to tell everyone, "You need to come over here and check this out!" which is sometimes followed by, "You're missing out if you don't come over here," and even, "What's wrong with you?! You didn't like it?" if someone comes along but it doesn't resonate as appropriate for them as it did for you.

Most interestingly, the wisdom teachers, around whose words and actions religions are constructed, were *never* exclusivist or exclusionary, and were in fact very loving and very INclusive in their words and actions. Many of today's faith communities claim to be welcoming, but I can say from personal experience that once I actually visited, I often found spoken or unspoken expectations around my existing belief system. I heard the term, "Loving admonishment," which was just a collective and agreed-upon set of rules that must be followed if one is to remain a member in good standing. I saw members with their own ideas of how life should be lived, who politely, or not-so-politely, asked me to worship elsewhere. Why does this appear to so frequently be the case? Are there any more potentially divisive, emotion-activating, preference-generating, expectation-filled realms than politics and religion? I was once told by a more liberal, more historically educated minister that the root of the word "heresy" meant "to think for one's self." God forbid!

Good news: Even in the heat of religious or political debate, we may, with practice, be the noticer of brain-generated thoughts about the person in front of us. We can notice how we perceive another person's ideas and ideologies and, in that noticing, come to understand more clearly the historical and cultural foundations that often lead to the belief systems to which people align. Even then, perhaps, we may still feel the need to challenge the beliefs of others. Be careful of who and how you're being in these moments! Our individual histories often yield resulting ideologies and philosophies that, regardless of how clearly we may distinguish them as subjective, nonetheless feel to us quite objective and deeply personalized. Can you imagine a more fertile ground for arguments?! What can we do?

Notice: When you recognize the concerns and divergent points of view, go within and apply your Point A and Point B awareness piece. Breathe. Smile. Remember that just as you are a valid soul standing in the awareness that you are, all souls are valid, even (and especially) the ones occupying bodies with brains that generate opinions that differ from yours. Remember, too, that within this context it's all about you! Your perceptions, your biases, your preferences, and your expectations are all based on your circumstances and history and resulting perception-filters. It's about your own amount of self-study, self-awareness, self-love, and self-forgiveness. Please remember that you cannot, at times, change your circumstances, but you can always change who you're being about them!

CHAPTER SEVENTEEN

PERSPECTIVES AND MORE APPLICATION OF THE REAL YOU PRINCIPLES

"It is what it is."

We've all heard this expression and know its implied connotation. "It is what it is" should be an objective statement, free of judgment or bias of any kind. It would, on the surface, imply acceptance and neutrality. Generally speaking, however, when people speak these words there is, more often than not, a sarcastic tone that generally has the phrase mean, "To heck with it (whatever "it" is)! This is as good as it's ever going to get, so I may as well just get over my preferences and desires of things ever changing. It is what it is!" This is, of course, anything but a neutrally expressed statement that usually wreaks of resignation, is inherently negative, and is not at all implying peaceful and pleasant acceptance of a person, place, or circumstance.

If we apply The Real You principles to this one, we can easily see that the common use of "It is what it is" shines a spotlight toward a Point B waiting to be explored, a moment of self-discovery in process, and an opportunity to send out some love and self-love, forgiveness and self-forgiveness!

If there's an "It is what it is" happening around you, or even something to be noticed within you, what is it? What might happen when you apply the Point A—Point B and resolve-refine-release processes to it? Are you in a place of neutral acceptance or are you actually in a place of preference-tainted, unfulfilled expectations, and darkened nonacceptance?

If we can willfully, intentionally, and consciously step back from resignation, hopelessness, and historically evidenced negativity to a place of actual neutral acceptance, we will find it easier to work our way from a neutral place to a peaceful and possibly even pleased state of being, instead of working from an inherently negative place up to neutral and then up to a positive state of being.

Remember that if we're basing any thoughts, opinions, or our present state of mind on something in our past, we may be letting that past experience filter our current perceptions. Remember that anything in your past happened in a "now moment" back then, and anything that ever will happen will happen in a "now moment" then. All we ever have is now. Both past and future are just brain-views that may be clouding our present. And if we are not in the awareness that we are, we may allow our thoughts to be filtered through the lens of that past or an anticipated future. If we can't look back in time at a particular person, situation, or circumstance without some "zingers" coming up —those twinges in our gut, back, or distractions when we go there—notice that! This is your body/mind/spirit telling you there is more work to be done in this area! Don't bury it or smooth it over with some habituated thought pattern used to justify burying it again, or some compensatory behavior that once served to distract or protect and get busy *now* applying The Real You principles to the issue.

The process may seem never-ending, as things will invariably continue to come up. You may be asking yourself "Am I ready to deal with this stuff?" A better question is, "Are you done dealing with it and ready to finally get it handled?" If that thing you thought you'd finished processing suddenly shows up again, because your always-thought-attaching brain successfully ties it together with some random thing you just saw or felt or heard or tasted, guess what? It's time for some more practice in The Real You principles! Don't worry. You're not alone!

I wrote this book, and I'm busy every day uncovering new messes I've left behind that still require some Point A—Point B, and resolve-refine-release work!

Here's another perspective: Consider the term "remember," or more specifically, to "re-member." A "member" might be a member in a group, as in a person "attached" to a group by membership. To "re-member" could apply to a part of our past that we bring back into the present moment and attaching it to our present-moment experience.

We must make any unresolved past experiences present in order to finally process through them. Remember the Iyanla Vanzant quote? We must make peace with our past and heal the wounds that occurred there. We must grow. We must evolve. Our spirits know the difference between being grounded in our self-work and a sense of false comfort derived from denying, suppressing, or lying to ourselves about our past. We can cover it over, but it all comes back to haunt us on some level, either in our minds or elsewhere in our bodies.

We must heal these wounds. We must make peace not with the people or experiences, as much as with who we've been being about those people and experiences. We must make peace, not with things we've done in our past, as much as with who we've been being about them. These are what we can change. We can always change who we've been being about it all, and we *must*. Always. Every Single Time. We can and we must if we are to finally clean up and be free from any physical and emotional stains left from our past. Likewise, we must free ourselves of any thoughts of the future that may be affected by our past experiences and present-moment concerns. In the Awareness that we are when we stand in The Real You place we can neutralize, if not eliminate these, one at a time.

All of these are handled when we are grounded in love and self-love, forgiveness and self-forgiveness, and awareness supported by The Real You principles. I know. "Simple, not easy," right?

We must stand in the place bigger than our circumstances.

We must stand in the place bigger than our thoughts about the circumstances.

We must stand in the place bigger than our emotions about the circumstances.

Notice, please, that it's about standing in the place that's bigger than all of these. Where is this place? Hint: when you die, and you're noticing the shell of your now dead body lying on the bed, floor, or wherever, it's the same place. Are you going to wait until you're dead to find this place? Life's certainly better if you find it sooner!

That place is found and experienced as we stand firmly grounded in the Awareness that we are, with forgiveness and self-forgiveness, washing away the long-carried and certainly burdensome mentally, emotionally, bodily, and spiritually painful pieces of our lives. We must untangle the proverbial rat's nest of messy internal wiring we've created in our lives until the brain-generated, bodily-experienced pain, anger, frustration, disappointment, and concerns eventually give way to a lasting peace—a peace blooming from the spiritual compost pile you've created through application of The Real You principles.

Once you've worked enough pieces of your life through the processes, your level of confidence in applying them will become the newly habituated way of being when the naturally-occurring "stuff happens." Instead of automatically flipping the switch of avoidance, denial, or suppression, you'll find yourself automatically flipping the noticer switch that leads into Point A—Point B, self-exploration, self-learning, self-forgiveness, and self-love. You'll become increasingly comfortable with embodying the courage, patience, and determination required to implement the resolve-refine-release process. The more you practice, the easier it gets. Myelination will become your friend, remember?

"Being in The Zone."

Remember those times when you were going for it freely, fully, and in flow? Those "in the zone" moments seem to happen only rarely to many of us, yet we see world-class athletes in every major sport, chess Grand Masters, even world-class chefs, get "into the zone" all the time! What's the difference between being "above average" and true greatness? There are few things that seem to be required: practice, loving what you do (enough to be willing to practice), and allowing the Presence that is already in you to come in and take over. The more myelinated The Real You principles become within you, the more readily and easily you will find it to drop into that place, and the easier it will be to stay "in the zone" yourself!

Practice is exactly what it sounds like, but any activity can be turned into a practice and a meditation: a tennis forehand, learning how to master throwing a curve ball, playing a musical instrument, typing on a computer keyboard, or what this book is all about—being the noticer of the thoughts your brain is generating, being the noticer of what's happening in your body, and being the noticer of what's happening all around you—and turning it all into a never-ending wealth of teaching material!

Loving what you do is "essential" as in at the fundamental, most basic essence-level of any activity or condition or thing of which we might speak. I don't mean patiently tolerating what you're doing, as in the possible feeling that "working" on grooving a forehand has become drudgery. I don't mean dealing with a work colleague's somewhat aggravating but tolerable personality, so you can be more focused at work. I'm not talking about liking when you're cleaning up around your home, where you may not be enjoying mopping the floor, but it needs to be done and you can see the difference it makes in the appearance of your kitchen or bathroom floor when you're done. I'm talking about loving what you're doing, as in being so in love and fulfilled by what you're doing that it becomes effortless, enjoyable, and rewarding in the very doingness of it. In doing that which you love, you literally feel better as you're doing it and still feel better afterward, knowing you've done it and done it well! On a more esoteric note, when you're living your fulfilled life as that which is Most You, you will, I promise you, touch other' lives and either reinforce their fulfilled path or inspire them to seek theirs for themselves! Remember the Chinese restaurant story and the owner who so loved his job that his love for his life literally infused his food and the atmosphere of the place with that? THAT! BE THAT!

Here's a practical living-your-life tip: if you're not spending time loving what you're doing at your job and/or with friends and family, and/or in any recreational activities in which you regularly participate, I really hope you get busy finding those things that truly light you up and turn you on. If you're noticing in this moment that you're at a loss for what that might be, notice that! This may be an indicator that you've lost touch with that which is Most You. If you can see you're in a rut that you've allowed yourself over time to ease into, you can, in the Awareness that you are, now extricate, forgive, and love yourself.

I watched my father make a very good living through which he provided admirably for our family, but I also watched him come in every night from his job and do the following: walk in through the back door, take his shoes off, take his belt off, take off his blazer, dress shirt, and tie (if he'd worn one that day), pull his tank-top t-shirt out of his pants, sit down in his chair, turn on the television, and sit silently and motionlessly watching whatever mindless game show or sitcom was on. Mom would fix dinner for us, and there were usually few words spoken or even allowed as dad watched TV. Sure, dad would crack a few "Dad jokes" during commercial breaks once he relaxed a bit, but if there were life problems to be discussed, we had two minutes and two seconds during the between-programs commercial breaks in which to share them before the next program segment came on. This lasted for the next several hours until it was our bedtime as kids or, when we were older, dad turned the TV off before going to bed. Five days a week for forty years.

Don't get me wrong, there were certainly places and activities that really turned my father on—serving in his Rotary Club and with Rotary International, our local Chamber of Commerce, his bowling league one night a week, and fishing with us kids (one or two Saturdays each month in the spring, summer, and fall) and with his fishing buddy (every Sunday for twenty years after he retired). The point is that for most of the week, at most of what he was doing, and for most of every day most of his life, who my dad was being while he was doing the doingness of his life was operating in an obligatory, soulless, bland, repetitive, and nonengaging fashion. He didn't hate what he was doing. He was brilliant at what he did, and it certainly opened many doors for him to share important parts of himself that needed to be shared. But he surely wasn't loving his job. For decades. Dad needed quadruple bypass surgery soon after his sixtieth birthday. Possibly a body affected by pained-heart beingness resulting in his heart trouble? I'd consider it possible.

It's never been about what you've been doing, it's always been about who you're being while you're doing it, who you're being about having to do it, and who you've been being about having done it.

Easier said than done, easier done than been.

"Holding Space."

We've all heard the term, "I'll be holding space for you." The term "holding space" implies holding an emptiness, which implies that none of our preferences, desires, needs, or wants are allowed in there. We must keep these out of the space or it's no longer empty! I know this seems obvious, but how many people practice "holding space" in this way? Not many, I'd wager.

"But what's the point of 'holding space' if we're not supposed to have any of our needs, wants, preferences, and desires in that space?" you may be asking. How do we manage to stay clear-headed during incidents with those we love most, and about which everything about the situation's preferred outcome is so very important to us? If it means that much, wouldn't we want to make our very best effort to make these moments as special as possible? Perhaps "effort" is exactly *not* the correct answer.

If "God is in the empty spaces," let's please allow Divinity to fill the space without our claiming to have any clue about how that's supposed to look. This may get easier to remember if we are seeking our heart's greatest desire, but if we are seeking whatever it is out of some egotistic drive to show off, to justify self-importance, or to make someone or something outside of us less important, something is most certainly awry.

Let's apply some noticing here to whatever it is that may have you "charged up." Notice that there *is* a charge—a strongly held preference for a given outcome—that may be overriding the clarity that always exists in The Real You place. As soon as we become aware of the charge, we can drop into The Real You place, see the Point B inherent in the charged preference, do some self-study, apply some resolve-refine-release process, and shift from charged to clear, from stressed to calm, from shifting sands of brain-generated discomfort amid uncertainty to the bedrock-beyond-circumstances that always lies just beneath the surface and that you've made more readily available through practicing The Real You principles.

We all want what we want, and we all want those we love to succeed, be happy, have good health, and know all of the other pieces of a beautiful life. This can make it challenging to remember this level of holding space. But I promise you, the results you seek will, in the long run, more readily occur when you do that type of space holding and be that type of space holder. Be the empty vessel through which Spirit may grant your greatest wish without you ever having to manage the details. Hold fast to the "what," and let that which is already in and all around you to manage the where/when/why/how/how much.

Think about sounds and frequencies. What differentiates a high-pitched sound from a low-pitched sound is its frequency. Take that word "frequency" literally for a moment. Frequency means "how often something is happening." In this case, it's how often a sonic waveform hits the eardrum in a given time period. The more often the frequency, the higher the note/tone/pitch. The less often the frequency, the lower the note/tone/pitch. Waveforms hitting the eardrum at 5000 times a second—5000 Hertz—make for a pretty high note. Waveforms hitting the eardrum at 30 times a second—30 Hertz—make for a very low note.

Here's the thing: It's still all about the empty spaces! Using the example above, 5000 peaks of a sonic waveform coming at the ear drum in one second requires very small spaces between the peaks. Thirty peaks of a sonic waveform coming at the eardrum in a second requires the spaces be much wider between the peaks. Different spaces for different sounds yielding different results, all as required in a given moment! Can we be empty vessels, allowing something far greater that ourselves to come through us as us?

"I am a hole in a flute that the Christ's breath moves through. Listen to this music."—Hafiz

Our favorite music is all about combinations of tones, either single notes or combinations of notes known as chords. Music has always fascinated me, and both of my brilliant sons have mastered multiple musical instruments. One is making a living as a musician and has been blessed to travel to many countries around the world sharing his musical talents. The other, while having as much raw musical talent as his brother, has a love of all things computers and excels in that arena.

One of the first things I taught both of my sons is that any given chord, regardless of the instrument on which it is played, instantly evokes an emotion. I discovered this in my own childhood while hacking around on our piano in our family living room and was fascinated by this phenomenon. I've since found that this chord-yields-emotion thing is universal, meaning that pretty much everyone I've met feels the same emotion when certain chords or chord combinations are played. "Haunting" chords sound haunting to everyone. "Inspiring" music is inspiring to everyone. If you pay attention to movie soundtracks, for example, you'll realize that the music playing in the background of a movie is what's actually generating the emotion you feel during the scenes! Want to know how crucial the music is? Pick out a really heavy scene in a movie, turn the sound off, and watch the people talking. The whole scene becomes almost comical. The soundtrack is an integral part of the feelings we experience as we're watching.

The point is that life is all about that which we choose to fill the empty spaces! Whether it's music filling the spaces in a movie, the food we eat that fills our bodies, or the information we ingest that fills our minds, the old expression of "garbage in, garbage out" could easily be rewritten, "fear in, fear out," "frustration in, frustration out," and "joy in, joy out."

Health is improved more by managing what consumes you than by managing what you consume.

- Brian Kurtz

Once again, The Real You principle of being the Awareness that we are allows us to notice and respond instead of mindlessly seeing and reacting. Mindful observation of what's happening in our brains, in our bodies, and in our daily lives provides a rich storehouse of experiential teaching material! Who will we be? How will we be? When will we begin practicing this? Now is as good a time as any to begin!

We can apply this mindful noticing—this "holding space"—to every aspect of our lives; not as some new neurotic obsession to replace another one, but rather as a consistent way of being to be implemented that improves our lives one ever-more-conscious moment at a time. When we have lunch at work, for example, are we filling that time slot with focus and intention on how our food is nourishing our bodies? Are we acknowledging the nourishment inherent in the food we're eating and the liquids we're drinking? Have we consciously chosen foods that are healthier and prepared by people who care about what they're providing?

These alone can up-level how we receive the nutritional value in what we consume. You can change this now if you so choose.

How about engaging more meaningfully—with eye contact that follows some "I" contact—the people around you in your workplace, at your kids' school, at the local coffee shop, or grocery store? Every aspect of every interaction can be an opportunity to operate in this new way of being. By being more often in the Awareness that you are, you share this way of being with others! You may be surprised at how differently people "occur" around you when you lovingly and with sincerity make eye contact with people around you! Try it and notice what happens!

Every single part of our day may be enhanced by this level of noticing and being. How about when we're sipping our morning coffee or tea . . . are you savoring every sip, or just unconsciously drinking it down while you check your phone, watch TV, or check out the latest podcast? What we choose to fill the empty spaces of our lives with, moment by moment—music, newscasts, talk shows, social media—as well as our conscious and subconscious thoughts in every piece of our lives are all crucial to how we feel about every facet of our lives, which often affect the results of our efforts.

"How are you doing today?"

If you find you have little or no energy after a rough day at work, notice the Point As and Point Bs about what you are able to discern in the noticing, and add some resolve-refine-release practice around it. Once you've cleared your mental/emotional plate a bit, stop and consider making the time to do something you really enjoy doing. The balance will improve your mental health as well as your physical health. Maybe that's exercise—being outdoors, talking a walk, or playing a sport—or perhaps what you need is a *non*active activity like reading an engaging book, fifteen to twenty minutes of meditation, or engaging some basic yoga poses—it really doesn't matter what it is you're doing, it's all about who you're being when you're doing it! Remember to notice the thought undercurrent that's flowing foundationally through your day, not as something to feed self-judgment, but as a way to facilitate your personal growth.

Want to be fulfilled at your job? Do you seek more intimacy, trust, respect, and vulnerability in your relationships with friends, family, and work colleagues? All of these have one crucial element in common: *being most you.* What is that "Most You" thing I keep mentioning? It's being as you as you can be, free from the effects of the unmet preferences and unfulfilled expectations, yielded through your practice that reveals your Point As and Point Bs, being more present more often to the Awareness that you are, and in diligently maintaining a perspective grounded in The Real You principles.

When something comes up that upsets you—especially those things you care most about—notice that! Stand in the place that's bigger than the circumstances or your opinions about them. Stand in the place that's bigger than your upset. Be the noticer! Practice The Real You principles, and I promise you that your life will slowly, possibly imperceptibly, but most certainly improve. You can also choose to blow all of this off, get back to "normal," and you already know what likely happens: you'll sense what you have perhaps often felt—disenchantment, disappointment, unconscious comparisons between what you have and what you prefer, and the resulting resignation, hopelessness, and inevitable sarcasm, denial, suppression, self-deprecation, self-medication or prescription medication—you know the list. These will, as reliably as the sunrise, devour your happiness, satisfaction, peace, and joy. Your call. Choose!

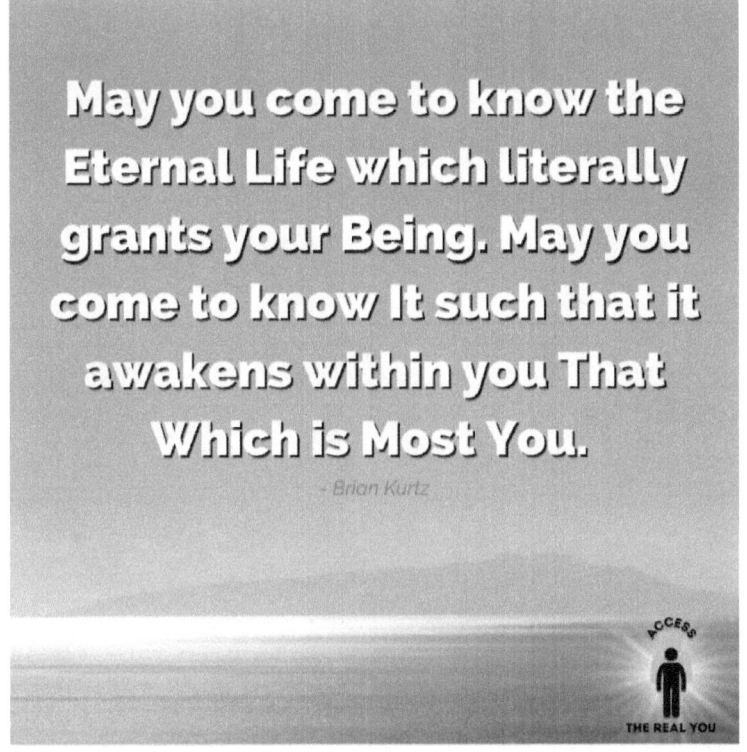

May you come to know the Eternal Life which literally grants your Being. May you come to know It such that it awakens within you That Which is Most You.

- Brian Kurtz

CHAPTER EIGHTEEN

AND WHAT OF CONFLICTS?

Conflict will arise. It must. If all is One, however, there can be no "conflict," only interaction that flows toward or farther away from resolution.

In conflict with another person, remember: Whose work is it? If the other person is being belligerent, argumentative, and or even passive-aggressively standoffish, there may be shared work, or there may be your work that is not at all the other person's work. Though complementary states of being may catalyze relationship and beauty, they may also catalyze conflict that, through its shared resolution, can serve to support both parties in becoming more enlightened, mature, trusting, and capable. "But what if the other person just doesn't even begin to see it as I do?" you may ask.

If you're unable to resolve an issue together, what might you refine about who you're being around the issue you couldn't resolve? Going deeper, what are the mind-generated agreements we have made in our lives, not just about that person but about people like that person, or circumstances that are similar to others you've encountered? Many of us have become so culturally ingrained in "the way things are" that we simply consider our interactions with them to be just "the way it is." But must it be that way?

Here are a few reminders of how deeply ingrained societal consciousness can change: In our own American history dark-skinned people were considered three-fifths of a human with regard to congressional representation. Women weren't allowed to vote. Renters of property were not allowed a vote or to hold elected office. Millions of First Peoples were exterminated. It may seem insane now, but that's how it was in a different time and place with different cultural norms and perspectives. The typical work week used to be sixty to eighty hours but got shortened significantly thanks to unions and workers collectively bargaining for more humane conditions. I know this history, yet when I owned my own retail business, I usually worked sixty to eighty to one hundred hours a week and considered that "just the way it is." With what possibly false conditions are you agreeing in your life? What is that inner, potentially unconscious agreement costing you in terms of your peace, happiness, and your overall level of self-actualization? How much of these are you willing to refine about yourself, and then, when you've done all you can and been all you can be about that subject, are you then willing to unconditionally release what remains?

I encourage you to ask the person in the mirror and wait for answers. We all deserve to be all we are here to be. If circumstances prevent you from having, doing, and being all your heart desires, look for new possibilities, new roles, new relationships, and new ways of being that facilitate, as opposed to hindering, your becoming Most You. Anything less than your best cheats yourself and everyone around you out of what you might otherwise contribute to our shared existence.

CHAPTER NINETEEN

THE REAL YOU PRINCIPLES APPLIED TO ROMANTIC RELATIONSHIPS

Relationships are the crucible for evolving every facet of your spiritual/emotional life. Everything that happens in a relationship can positively impact your well-being if you let the relationship guide you and not allow it to become a brain-generated justification for self-torment and frustration. Every thought and every unconscious brain-generated outpouring can be influential! Shared consciousness and deep connection are wonderful, but it is precisely this deep connection that, when conflict does arise, can bring out both the best and the worst in us—usually, precisely because we care so much!

Vulnerability—sharing your deepest and most heartfelt feelings and desires—is a key component in any relationship. These are often, of course, the most frightening pieces of yourself, your life history, and your most frightening emotions to share with your romantic partner, because sometimes you may not know how your partner will react! As mentioned with regard to interpersonal relationships in general, if you're not willing to risk the relationship to share that which is Most You, you're cheating your partner out of the opportunity to know you better, and you're cheating yourself out of the opportunity to be all you are. I know this can be downright scary, but I encourage you to risk it all!

I belong to an international men's organization called The Mankind Project (mkpusa.org). I'm told there are now over 75,000 men in over forty countries who've participated in their work, which brilliantly combines indigenous ceremony with Jungian archetypal concepts. The "MKP" program supports men in safely, securely uncovering their deepest wounds, to help them come to know what's been missing in their lives and to transform these formerly missing pieces into mission statements and supported plans of action to bring to their world what's been absent in their lives. "Mature masculinity" is so very necessary in our world, as opposed to the toxic males seen on the news and reality TV shows. The late George Carlin, one of the funniest comedians, as well as one of the most incisive judges of human nature I've ever heard, once said "Women are crazy and men are stupid, and the reason women are crazy is because men are stupid." Most marriages between average American humans, who may not have done a lot of inner or interpersonal work, generally result in contributions to the high divorce percentages (me included, which is why I've worked long and hard to uncover and resolve issues, refine who I've been being about those unresolvable issues, and lovingly release what remains).

I freely admit that it is only in the last decade or so, as a middle-aged man that I'd be willing to seriously entertain marriage again, and only with a partner totally committed to our personal growth and the growth of "Us" as a unit. I've tried and "failed" so many times, but I've never given up trying. What was missing in the past was MY work on myself and MY work in the relationship. In every one of my last several relationships, each of which lasted a few years, I was simply unable or unwilling to be who my partner needed me to be. Either I felt like I had to get used to "not getting my way," or I witnessed what I considered dysfunction that, after my last failed marriage, I would never consciously allow to remain unchecked and unresolved. I committed to never stop doing my own work on myself and my own work within the relationship. I committed to being with potential partners who were equally committed to doing their own work, as well as our work within the relationship. As a result, even when those relationships "didn't make it," most ended peacefully and respectfully between friends.

Most of the long-term relationships I've witnessed are not at all those with which I'd be satisfied, but I most certainly acknowledge the patience, courage, and obvious loving commitment shared by couples who make it through twenty, thirty, or forty years or more of marriage. The few couples I've seen who've remained happy for all those years have done years of therapy, couples and individuals coursework, etc., to keep things open, fresh, and exciting. Lots of work and lots of play are pretty much mandatory for a successful relationship in today's ever-more-complex world.

I could likely write another entire book about applying The Real You principles to relationships, but let's cover the basics here. It's never been about our past relationships or the people with whom we were involved, rather it's always been about who we've been being about them, the shared circumstances, and the emotions we still carry about it all. It's about who you've been being and who you're being now, to which I encourage you to apply the Real You principles until you're able to notice your past as passed and your present simply occurring around you.

And what of present relationships? Same thing, of course! The work to be done in a current relationship never starts with the other person but with you. It's always about you. It's never about the other person or about "how they make you feel." It's more about noticing how you feel when you witness certain behaviors or expressions, or hear certain phrases, or feel into the other person's Presence, or notice that you're experiencing certain feelings and perceptions about the person in front of you that may have nothing directly to do with them, and everything to do with the person you see (or avoid seeing) in the mirror every day.

The courage to be vulnerable is an inside job. Breaking through old behavior patterns that may once have served us and replacing these with new ways of being is challenging work, often requiring the support of trusted and well-trained therapists and facilitators of improved and integrated experience. Your current set of nonromantic relationships may not include those trusted friends, trained therapists, and other resources to support your discovery of issues to notice, with whom to work through the Point As and Point Bs and to work through the resolve-refine-release process. In that case, you'll need to practice even more diligently The Real You principles.

These foundational Real You principles are essential to living your best life as an individual, as well as to live your best joined life with your partner. The work is the same as your individual work, but now it will be critical that you remember you're working with not only your own Point As and Point Bs but also your partner's Point As and Point Bs, and the Point As and Point Bs within the joined aspects of your relationship itself. Again, this applies not only for you but for your partner, and even in the "Us" that's almost like a separate entity that you are cocreating together. This becomes extremely complicated and requires much patience on the part of both partners since the discovery process constantly evolves, and never really ends. Both of you must remain in a state of Awareness and Presence, ever mindful of what's going on in your respective brains, in your bodies, and in the world around each of you and with both of you (I could write an entire book on this last sentence alone and just might write that follow up someday). It's essential that you support your partner in doing and being the same, not only making time to discuss and identify what may be happening to/within each of you, but also to discuss and identify what that "Us" looks like with the two of you as partners.

Remember that this is also made more complicated by the fact that there are at least four dynamics taking place during any conversation:

*You about your own stuff

*Your partner's stuff about his/her/their own stuff

*Your stuff about your partner's stuff

*Your partner's stuff about your stuff

And this "stuff" can be floating around in each of your heads, based in historical experiences with each other, from each of your past relationships, or include family and/or parental or work-related relationships, or not-yet-occurring expected experiences in a future that haven't even happened yet. These are often based in some past events or in an interpretation of something that has something or nothing to do with the thoughts each or both of your brains may be generating about that future experience, or any of these in the other person's brain, whether being noticed or not, and whether they're accurate or not, and whether they're even real or not.

UGH, right? Is your head swimming?! Notice that! Remember the thought undercurrent? Here's another possible piece of that. Notice how you might be judging yourself: "I am too tall, too short, not smart enough, not as sharp as I was twenty years ago, too fat, I look wrinkly and old, my hair's gone gray," or whatever Point A "what's so" you can compare to your Point B's preference. If any preferences are unshared, not agreed upon with your partner, and remain unresolved, these issues might ultimately become walled-off life aspects into which you place yourself securely to avoid conflict, thus limiting your way of being in the world! As long as we attach our identities to these boxes into which we place ourselves and about which we become complacent or resigned, we remain trapped there.

Now, mirror all of that for your partner! We've all built walls into our very existence by the perceptions we hold about ourselves within our world and relationships, romantic or otherwise. Complex? YES! There's still some good news, however: In the very awareness of and acknowledgment of the existence of these walls and commitment to work through them with your partner, they may be eliminated! Of course, there are many such boxes, and all are able to be worked through to get to a better relationship, and thus a better life, regarding every one of them!

As in the *Matrix* movie, we are trapped in an illusory reality that this book is intended to make more and more obvious with distinctions that reveal brain-generated thoughts that may have influenced our perceptions and thus our very reality. By standing in the ever-evolving, ever-growing, ever-loving, ever-forgiving Awareness that we are, we may, as relationship partners, take baby steps, then larger steps, then find ourselves running freely together in a new reality that we are able to create for ourselves and for the "Us" into which our relationships may evolve!

CHAPTER TWENTY

EXERCISES AND PRACTICES

Look into a mirror. Don't look away. Stare into your own eyes and keep staring. I know it's just a book. Put the book down after you read the next few paragraphs and just go and do it! Notice what occurs. You may get impatient, sad, angry, insecure, or a host of other emotions, distractions, or other previously generated and practiced behaviors, or thought patterns designed to prevent making that "I" contact. DO IT ANYWAY, PLEASE! Go to the mirror now (no, really! do it and do it now!) and ask the person in the mirror:

"How are you doing?"

After you've practiced The Real You principles for a while, here are some "graduate-level" questions to ask yourself as you stand before yourself in the mirror:

"Am I ready to be the full depth and breadth that I am?"

"Do I have the courage to fully embody The Real Me? Do I have the 'the heartage?' Can I live this new way second by second, minute by minute, hour by hour, day by day, for as often as I can, as deeply as I can, and forgive myself the rest?"

There are messes I've made that I've carried in my heart, soul, and in the actual physical cells in my body *for decades.* Not just small mistakes, either; big mistakes. Mistakes that cost me a job. Mistakes that harshly impacted others' lives as well as my own. My not living up to my end of the financial bargain for years, which cost me a marriage and a couple of other relationships. Not even so much about what my partner thought about me, though that contributed, as much as *what I thought about me*. The self-torment, self-doubt, and self-loathing were devastating, gripping, and relentless. I awoke every morning for several years with my bed drenched in my own sweat. My back ached. My knees ached. My brain and body were exhausted before I had even started my day. As with many successful people I've met and with whom I've had conversations, I'm still surprised at how many people have been through this. Knowing you are not alone may not help much, but at least you know.

The only solution I've found? Self-love and self-forgiveness. Simple, not easy, if we attempt to let the brain figure a way to justify the conditions and state of conditionality that same brain created for us to traverse in order to be worthy of that self-forgiveness. Here's the big question to ask yourself: "*Have I paid the price sufficiently by now to allow myself to be free of it and walk forward from here?*" Your answer to this one sets the tone of the thought undercurrent that to some extent runs you until you're aware that it's not The Real You.

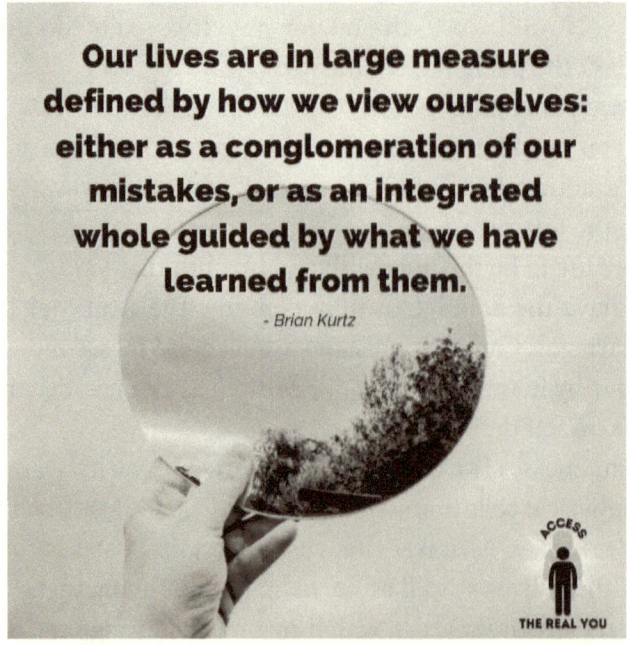

Our lives are in large measure defined by how we view ourselves: either as a conglomeration of our mistakes, or as an integrated whole guided by what we have learned from them.

- Brian Kurtz

In a crisis, what are we to do? Who are we to be? By now you know that my recommendation any time you find yourself in overwhelm, instead of trying to "figure" a way out or a way to survive the situation (which requires using the brain, which we now know is often the problem) is always to get back to The Real You basics.

Breathe in to five and out to eight, four or six or even eight times. This activates and maintains a major relaxation response in the vagus nerve that touches all major organs in the body. Next, of course, is to smile—this always works because it, too, triggers a vagus nerve relaxation response! Now, given that you're likely already at least a bit better than you were five minutes ago, step back and notice your brain. The thoughts likely racing through it contain every conceivable, historically-relevant event the brain can possibly generate in far-better-than-record time. Let them go, at least until you're back in a mental/emotional space to start processing the Point As and Point Bs of it all. Once you've identified those, it's still both appropriate and effective to start singling out individual issues for resolve-refine-release. This whole exercise will give your brain far more productive work to do than drag-racing your beingness into panic-driven oblivion. The Real You is always bigger than your brain chatter and always bigger than the circumstances about which your brain chatter is screaming.

Next, notice your body. It may be feeling generally tense and charged up, though sometimes some of us go a bit numb, in which case you may feel nothing. Or you may feel like you just took a punch to the gut, or perhaps your head is aching or your back is spasming. Any and all of these are fine when you can remember you are not your body but are the noticer of whatever it's feeling in the moment. The Real You is always bigger than whatever the body is feeling, thus you can, with practice, notice and work bioenergetically with what comes up on your body.

Here's an exercise to help you begin to directly work with what you may encounter in your body:

- Feel into your body. Identify where you're feeling what you're feeling in your body.

- Visualize the following, if you're one who can do that:
  - o Open a small hole in front of you, perhaps a foot or two wide.
  - o Encapsulate the bodily area of concern in a bubble of light.
  - o Reach into your body, guide the bubble out of your body, and drop it into the hole in front of you.
  - o Visualize light pouring from a space above you into the hole.
  - o Close the hole.

This next one may sound totally insane to some of you but try it and see what happens. It's another fun symbolic visualization that is the "blessing" I place on my food before eating or drinking anything.

- As I inhale, I pull light from Mother Earth below me, through my body, up and over me connecting to Spirit above me.
- As I exhale, I pour that light down on to my food and beverage.
- I inhale again, drawing upward and above me the energy from my now-lit-up food and drink.
- I exhale again, and pour that raised energy from my food and drink downward into my body, nourishing me energetically before I ever ingest the food and drink.

This simple visualization leaves me feeling better after every meal!

Finally, notice as often as possible what's happening around you. The circumstances may, in fact, be very much worthy of your time and energy, but never worthy of your stressing about them. Once you're in a place of peace and perspective, step back to a physical, mental, emotional, and perhaps spiritual distance from the stressors until you feel a bit more under control and ready to get to the next step.

Ask these questions throughout the day:

- What is my brain generating about what is occurring around me?
- What am I feeling about what is occurring around me?

- What am I to learn from this experience?

- What might I learn about myself as I interact with people and circumstances showing up in my awareness at this moment?

- How might all of these thoughts, feelings, people, and experiences serve me as I stand in The Real You place?

- As I "zoom out," noticing all of this, is there some place in my larger perspective and broader and deeper awareness in which all of these thoughts, feelings, people, and experiences are able to be placed into a single, larger contest that contributes to my feeling a part of the Oneness in which my life may be experienced?

For now, these questions may seem rather odd. Practicing The Real You principles may transform them from confusing to enlightening. If your brain isn't pleased with the short-term or long-term results, remember you are not your brain, you are the noticer of it! It gets easier, I promise!

CHAPTER TWENTY-ONE

WORDPLAY

hope you find these interesting. I've long enjoyed playing with words and studying them in hopes of "dis-covering" deeper meaning in their etymology and getting creative in their usage so that I may "realize" their wider applicability to me and my life. This chapter is all about enhancing perspective. I hope it serves!

There's plenty of fun to be had in such wordplay. For example, notice that a little space completely changes, even reverses, the meanings of words.

The difference between "nowhere" and "now here" is a little space.
- Brian Kurtz

Nowhere = nonexistent,   Now here = present

Apart = separate, A part of = together

The root "trans" means "across," as in to change or move from one form or place to another. If our awareness stops here, we end up with two of whatever it may be:

TRANSportation is getting from one place to another.

TRANSgender is changing from one gender to another.

TRANSform is to change form from one thing to another (caterpillar into butterfly, for example, not merely changing some aspect, like color).

TRANSmit is to send a message from one place to another.

What if we were more inclusive in our perspective about these words? Suddenly we can see that:

Transportation is a single journey between two places.

Transgender pertains to a single person who is changing between two genders.

Transform applies to one thing that's transformed from one thing into something completely different.

Transmit applies to a single and complete idea transmitted between two locations.

All of these on the surface may comprise two apparently distinct parts—a beginning and an ending, a starting place and a stopping place—but they are actually joined within and through the process. The unifying awareness of the wholeness grants a perspective that is larger than, more complete than, and more expansive than the mere noticing of dualistic, separated parts like "a beginning and an end."

CONgress—gathering as a whole

CONtract—agreement between parties working together

CONflict—disagreement between parties trying to work together

CONtact—coming together or engagement between separate people

As we expand our perspective to be more inclusive, the more broadly we will see all that awaits us in that new and more expansive and inclusive awareness.

The more often and more readily we make the time and mind space to "zoom out"—taking our noses off the proverbial grindstone—we are able to see with a broader perspective that in and of itself may, in the psychological/emotional space generated in the awareness, grant us more peace along our journey. Seeing obstacles immediately in front of us—when our perception is one of noticing from a stepped back place—may become merely obstacles to get *through* to get *to* our destination or goals. We may apply this inherently unifying perspective to any and every aspect of our lives, which might otherwise yield brain-generated worries, doubts, and concerns for our brains to "figure out" that, in all likelihood, simply keep us stuck in the mindset that is generating the problem in the first place!

CHAPTER TWENTY-TWO

GRAVITY—AFFECTING CHANGE JUST BY BEING MOST YOU

This may be getting a bit esoteric and may even seem a bit pointless to some of you, but here goes.

Have you ever noticed the foam bubbles in a cup of coffee? The smaller groups of bubbles get pulled into the larger ones. If you've never noticed this phenomenon, try it sometime. Stir up your coffee and watch what happens. The smaller bubbles get pulled into the larger ones, the smaller groups get pulled into the larger ones, and the edge of the cup draws all of it into the sides. The same thing applies to consciousness and "group think." The more bubbles, or minds, or amount of consciousness that become aligned to a particular purpose, the more powerful the result will always be. This can, I believe, apply to the spread of ideas and momentum of this spreading of ideas. The "100th monkey" story illustrates how powerful this phenomenon can be! Quoting Wikipedia about this:

Between 1952 and 1953, primatologists conducted a behavioral study of a troop of Macaca fuscata (Japanese monkeys) on the island of Kōjima. The researchers would supply these troops with such foods as sweet potatoes and wheat in open areas, often on beaches. An unanticipated byproduct of the study was that the scientists witnessed several innovative evolutionary behavioral changes by the troop, two of which were orchestrated by one young female, and the others by her sibling or contemporaries. The account of only one of these behavioral changes spread into a phenomenon (i.e., the 'hundredth monkey effect'), which Watson would then loosely publish as a story.

According to Watson, the scientists observed that some of the monkeys learned to wash sweet potatoes, initially through an 18-month-old female member (named "Imo" by the researchers) of the troop in 1953. Imo discovered that sand and grit could be removed from the potatoes by washing them in a stream or in the ocean. Gradually, this new potato-washing habit spread through the troop—in the usual fashion, through observation and *repetition*. (Unlike most food customs, this behavior was learned by the older generation of monkeys from younger ones.)

This behavior spread up until 1958, according to Watson, when a sort of group consciousness had suddenly developed among the monkeys, as a result of one last monkey learning potato washing by conventional means (rather than the one-monkey-at-a-time method prior). Watson concluded that the researchers observed that, once a critical number of monkeys was reached—i.e., the hundredth monkey—this previously learned behavior instantly spread across the water to monkeys on nearby islands.

Watson first published the story in a foreword to Lawrence Blair's Rhythms of Vision (1975); the story then spread with the appearance of Watson's 1979 book Lifetide: The Biology of the Unconscious.

The hypothetical point to be made here is that just by being Most You, being all you're here to be, it's possible that you will become more tapped in to your own higher states of Being and in so doing you may not only attract others of a similar mindset, but potentially impact others' consciousness. At some point, the larger community's consciousness might be impacted, and a sort of idea-momentum begins to spread on its own! I've had many such experiences where I had an idea and found out a few days later that friends had the same idea in the same general time frame! My own "Adam and Eve" story mentioned previously came to me on the same day and at the same time as a minister friend of mine had received it. When I met him the following Sunday and shared it with him, it turned out that his experience had yielded exactly the same content and exact same context shared in that Sunday's sermon that he'd been preparing all week to deliver!

The Divine Wisdom available to all of us is floating around in the ether ready for someone to tune in to that frequency and receive it. As one might tune in to a radio station whose information is being carried along a specific frequency, all we have to do is tune in and listen.

What most serves you? What most turns you on? What feels like Most You?

Always look for what there is for you to have, to do, and to be. That which is Most You and Most Yours is always worth seeking, and these parts of you and your life are what *pulls* you forward into your life, even in times of great challenges, as opposed to the difficulties in life that we might say we most want or most need, and yet we often find ourselves having to *push* through them. Instead of pushing and enduring and efforting, how many people can you bring along with you if you invite them to *play* with you instead of gathering to *work* with you? If you can gather like-minded people who are as excited as you are about these activities, go for it! You'll find added momentum in the gravity inherent in the like-mindedness! It will be the same activity, only now you'll likely experience it with a greatly improved and collectively shared attitude!

You may be asking, "How do we do that? How do we "tune in" to the correct frequency?" Remember that this "place" is the same place where love comes from, from which music and poetry flow and connect us to others within earshot (and perhaps, "soulshot"), and the place from which all of the best things in life emanate. Have you ever truly loved someone? Have you ever had an epiphany that just lit you up, catalyzing profound change in your life and life-path? Have you ever had those moments of "being in the zone" where everything just effortlessly fell into place as if by magic? This is the place I'm talking about!

The flipside of this "spread the love" and its "gravity" concept is that we can also radiate anger, fear, hatred, and pain. Eckhart Tolle talked about what he called "the pain body" and how unconsciously contagious that could be. The good news is that heartfelt love and our Divine Presence is always more powerful, so have no fear. If you feel a negative vibe, be aware of it, do not fear it, and stand in the loving and powerful Presence of The Real You. Once again, who you're being in The Real You place is bigger than any person or circumstance.

Here's a tip regarding manifestation and the extent to which "the frequency to which you're tuned in" might facilitate manifestation of your most heart-felt desires: if you're a bit "off-frequency," but you mean well, that's still usually plenty! You'll be attracting into your presence that which most accurately reflects what you're out-projecting. I find that when I'm ready to attract more clients, more income, and more of life's blessings, those things occur more readily! If I'm a little off-center in my attitude and grounding, good things still occur, if not exactly as I might have expected. I've found, for example, that when I'm making calls to connect with my clients in an effort to add to my business through the service I provide, what invariably happens is that although I may get some "no thanks" or "it's not time for me to work with you again just yet" responses, I still get calls during this same time frame from clients who are ready to work with me, even if I hadn't even thought of them in any conscious way! The result still happens, even though not quite as I'd planned. This always seems to work! What you seek you will find! The only exception I've found in this is when that aforementioned "meaning well" might hurt someone in some real way.

The problem I see in dogmatic religious practice (or any activity in which enthusiasm and fervor-enhanced group-think is prevalent), for example, is that those who participate in ways that are inherently dogmatic and inflexible are often condescending, rude, and even dangerous to those who believe or perceive matters differently, even though those well-intentioned zealots really do "mean well."

We've all heard the stories of anti-abortion activists bombing women's health centers and religious zealots bombing houses of worship. Clearly, this is nothing more than insanity justified within perversely twisted priorities. When religious fervor gets out of control, violence becomes more possible. Domestic terrorism is at its highest rate since the American Civil War. There are more mass shootings in the United States than any other developed nation on earth. For all the cultural awareness around such violence, few seem willing to admit there are underlying long-term factors such as social, racial, and economic injustice fueled by longstanding bigotry that fuel new incidents. Mass protests, both violent and nonviolent, have become commonplace, and the issues about which they are formed must be resolved before matters will improve meaningfully.

While I do not approve of violence of any kind, I believe the violence and division are to some extent required for long-term resolution. Underlying conflicts must come to the surface before they can be resolved. We can sweep things under the proverbial rug, but the lump underneath becomes a mound in the middle of our living room if we don't finally address the problems.

I'm not trying to get political here, rather I'm trying to make a point: What's the one thing all of these forms of hate, violence, polarization, and misplaced overzealousness have in common? They all occurred, I'd wager, when people were nowhere near their head-space and heart-space of practicing or even being aware of The Real You principles! Wherever such polarization and reactionary entrenchment exist, I assure you that what fuels the fire is brain-justified division, brain-justified violence, and brain-generated reactionary rhetoric that have nothing to do with love, inclusion, peace, awareness and self-awareness, love and self-love, forgiveness and self-forgiveness.

What can you do, and who can you be when you find yourself feeling angry, frustrated, frightened, or trapped in such circumstances? I strongly recommend being Present, standing in the Awareness that you are, and practicing the beautiful grounding inherent in The Real You principles. I know of no other way that is as effective and as efficient in producing both short-term and long-term inner peace, and that enhances the possibility of making impactful "I" contact and eye contact in the midst of conflict.

We must not just *do* better. We must *be* better, and we can, regardless of circumstances. If you don't think we can, notice that. You are not the thinker, you are the noticer of the thoughts thought by the thinker. That noticer is The Real You. Be that. Be there. Be.

CHAPTER TWENTY-THREE

NOW WHAT?

If you've been paying attention and practicing what's available in this book, you've no doubt learned a lot, and I don't mean more stuff for your brain to store for later. The more you practice The Real You principles and apply them to what your brain is generating moment-by-moment, the more conscious you can become—with the Awareness that you are—of who you're being about whatever brain generated thoughts are occurring to be noticed. The more you practice The Real You principles and apply them to what you're noticing in your body moment-by-moment, the more conscious you can become—with the Awareness that you are—of what your body has to tell you about who you're being about what may be occurring to be noticed. The more you practice The Real You principles and apply them to what's occurring around you, the more conscious you can become—with the Awareness that you are—of who you're being about what's occurring around you to be noticed.

There is no end to the process of applying The Real You principles to every aspect of your life, because life continues until the day The Real You transitions out of your body on to whatever is next. In the meantime, who you're being about it all makes all the difference, and that can be magnificent or horrible, as you so choose. By now, it should be clear that the choice is yours. Not your brain's choice but yours, as in The Real You's choice!

Is this the end of the beginning or the beginning of the end? The answer to that is contained in more questions:

Who is the one who wants to know? Where is that one who wants to know? Why does it matter to the one who wants to know? The one to whom it matters is not The Real You. That which wants to know, needs to know, and must know is not The Real You. The Real You already knows. The Real You has always known and will always know. On this you can most certainly depend. The problem is getting what's not The Real You out of the way.

The nature of Being is beyond words adequate to fully describe it. There's a word that someone created just for this: ineffable. It's opposite, effable, means "capable of being uttered or explained; able to be spoken of; able to be expressed." Indeed, Beingness may be momentarily touched, and we may know it as it's experienced, but it cannot be completely held by our brains that want so desperately to "understand" that which cannot be fully understood, and so tightly grasp and hold on to opinions used to justify whatever upset they can generate about anything and everything thought or experienced.

The Hebrew language, as I understand it, has no word for the present-tense form of "to be." In other words, there is no "is," or "am." When one considers that the Judeo-Christian Bible says that, when Moses thanked the Presence in the burning bush for providing all of the wonderful information that had been delivered, and then asked the Presence for Its name, It is said to have transmitted the words, "I am that I am." If Hebrew has no such word, the best that could have been communicated was, "I me" or something to that effect. The best we can do is to touch various aspects of this Beingness, as I've attempted to do in this book. Remember the laser pointer and coffee mug analogy? The same is with Beingness. Until we've experienced it, we can't truly know it, and even after we have experienced it we are at a loss to adequately describe it. Beingness is so elusive that, even in the middle of our experiencing it we will lose that state as soon as our brains start to congratulate us on arriving there! As soon as we exclaim to ourselves or to anyone present, "I'm there!" it is, by definition, gone, for the ego can't Know Beingness, it can only know It as a concept. The best the brain can make of it is to generate a memory of the experience, but the fullness can only be experienced in the "now" and not in a "then."

Once we Know that we Know, there's no need to explain it, to justify our conclusion or experience of it, or any other such behavior or thought patterns. In the realm of that which we Know that we Know, all simply *is*, and as much as our brain would like to drop that Knowing into a parsed segment of brain synapses, Beingness is incapable of being stored for later. The brain can only compare vaguely that Beingness experience to something in the past (that happened in a Now moment then) *or* hoped for in a future that won't exist until a Now moment then.

The opportunity to exist in the Now lives in everyone always. We need only step back from our brain chatter about what's happening in our brains, in our bodies, and in our surrounding circumstances, and simply Notice it all. Simple, not easy. Easier said than done, easier done than been.

From this noticer place, the real adventure begins! Go be you! Being anything less cheats us all out of who you're here to be, and cheats yourself out of all you're here to experience, learn, do, and be. In the Grand Path, as it were, there are no poor choices, only lessons. If we get off center, we'll be guided back, either through subtle coaxing and revealed Knowing or, if we're too stubborn, by a few good slaps, kicks, or outright knockdowns in life that will likely occur because the Spirit you are, which is The Real You, will on some level generate those growth experiences and lessons for your brain and 3D body. I know I've experienced these at one time or another, and though I'd prefer subtle whispers in my ear, I have no regrets about the times I was "knocked conscious." All in a day's work, or play, such as the case may be. Who we're being about it makes all the difference!

Please discover for yourself what you truly love doing and do as much of it as you can. Pour out your soul into whatever that is for you, and you will find that you will feel better, be more energized, more pleased with yourself and what's happening around you, and generally be more satisfied with your life—not as something else for which your ego can pat you on the back, but as a more enlightened and enlivened way of being!

Keep noticing! Keep learning! Keep evolving! It's all already in there, awaiting your arrival to the place of Awareness where all is shown and Known. Best wishes on your walk through your world of true self-help!

ACKNOWLEDGEMENTS

I wish to acknowledge some very special people who have profoundly impacted my life in ways which got me to the place where this book was finally written:

To my sons, Asher and Jonathan, who are my most cherished humans, and who have brought me immeasurable joy and satisfaction, and to their mothers who, by being both that which I'd preferred and that which I'd not preferred, have taught me much, and with whom our shared challenges have become for me profound and lasting teaching material.

To Jennifer Harrison-Sanchez, whose friendship and constant encouragement provided much needed inspiration in the actual writing and completion of this book. Simply stated, this book would likely never have been completed without her coming into my life when she did and providing much appreciated support throughout its writing. THANK YOU.

To Deidre Stratton, whose shared truly extraordinary Divine Connection has allowed me to ongoingly refine my knowledge of and grounding myself in how to most effectively apply The Real You principles to every aspect of my daily life, THANK YOU.

To my dear friends and to the thousands of clients who have participated in my workshops where The Real You conversation has been refined and presented, THANK YOU.

To my Brothers in The Mankind Project who have supported and participated in my workshops, and who allowed me to present my workshop to the USA Gathering of Elders, THANK YOU.

To those whose direct support made publishing this book possible: Penny Small, Karen Roberts, Margaret Bohn, Kevin and Victoria Faith McIntyre, Stephanie Harrover, Douglas and Peggy Klein, Cedric Meza, Robin Kurtz-Lendner, and Jennifer Harrison-Sanchez, FOR ALL YOU ARE FOR ME, BLESS YOU AND THANK YOU ALL.

To fellow author Stacie Ivey who, after hearing The Real You conversation for the first time, exclaimed "THIS NEEDS TO BE A TED TALK!" which served to inspire me to continue on my way toward refining The Real You principles, THANK YOU!

I wish to thank most sincerely my writing coach and provider of many meaningful experiences over the last several years, Amy Collette, who not only provided fertile ground from which to sow the seeds of wisdom and achievement represented by this book, but provided constant nourishment of ideas through her ongoing enthusiastic support, and for providing me the ticket of a lifetime: to attend Alexandra Agresta's "Purpose Pioneers" Thought Leader Conference, where the seed-thought of "IT'S TIME TO BRING THIS BOOK TO THE WORLD!" came to be.

Lastly and most importantly, I express my most sincere gratitude for That Which Sources My Being, such that these words have come through me as me for you. I hope it serves!

ABOUT THE AUTHOR

Brian Kurtz is an intuitively-guided medical empath whose commitment to service is the common thread in his life's work. After many years as a professional recreation programmer and decades in the consumer electronics industry, Brian has dedicated his life to healing and energy work. He started receiving divine downloads almost forty years ago that have facilitated his personal growth into who he is today—a healing vessel and teacher who calls in Spirit's power and love to heal physical, psychological, and emotional issues.

Kurtz is also speaker and author, as well as a dedicated father to his two sons. His mission is to contribute to the ongoing global spiritual awakening that will someday render pointless the brain-generated barriers we humans create between ourselves and others.

Access The Real You is Brian's first book. Accompanying volumes for young children, adolescents, and couples are in the works!